THE SACRED DANCE OF SOUL

THE SACRED DANCE OF SOUL

YOUR INNER JOURNEY TO EMPOWERMENT

MADELINE K ADAMS

ROSLYN PUBLISHING

Copyright © 2019 by Madeline K Adams

All rights reserved. This book or any portion thereof may not be reproduced or used in any manner whatsoever; Other than for 'fair use' as brief quotations embodied in articles and reviews, without prior written permission of the publisher

The information given in this book should not be treated as a substitute for professional medical advice. Any use of information in this book is at the reader's discretion and risk. The intent of the author is only to offer information of a general nature to help the reader in their quest for soul wellbeing. Neither the author nor the publisher can be held responsible for any loss, claim or damage arising out of the use, or misuse, of suggestions made, the failure to take medical advice, or for any material on third party websites.

First Published September 2019

A catalogue record of this book is held at the National Library of New Zealand
ISBN: 978-0-473-48720-1
ISBN: 978-0-473-51266-8

Roslyn Publishing Limited
P O Box 32276
Auckland, 0744
New Zealand

Cover Image: Johny Goerend
Aurora Borealis, Norway
Cover Design: Jesh art studio

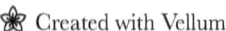 Created with Vellum

To those who feel invisible

Find the courage to follow your heart

And shine the true light of your soul

CONTENTS

Prologue — 1
Introduction — 7

PART I
1. The Pure Essence of the Feminine — 13
2. Becoming an Awakened Soul — 17
3. Soul Wisdom — 20

PART II
4. Catalysts for Transformation — 27

PART III
5. The Myth of Persephone — 45
6. Persephone – an Empowered Woman — 51

PART IV
7. Becoming Visible, Stepping into a New Story — 63

PART V
8. Soul Laws of Living — 77
9. The Power of the Great Unconscious — 83

PART VI
10. Soul life of a Modern Mystic — 97
11. A New World View — 103

PART VII
12. Happiness and Connection to Source — 111
13. Creativity, Imagination and Art — 118
14. A Creatress Blessing — 128

PART VIII
15. Creatress Practices 133
16. Soul Therapy for a Creatress 143
17. Reminising's 150

Acknowledgments 157
Sources and Other Reading 159
Also by Madeline K. Adams 163
Postscript 165
About the Author 167

"Beauty is truth, truth beauty"
That is all ye know on earth
And all ye need to know"

~ John Keats
Ode on a Grecian Urn

PROLOGUE

Many years ago, I traveled to the South West of France, on a journey that became the catalyst for my soul awakening. It was in France that I heard the call to dance with my soul and I discovered the aliveness of my awakened heart.

My first memory of the presence of my Soul was the day I started ballet lessons at the age of four. Dancing touched something deep within my heart, opening me to a new world and giving me an outlet to express the whole of myself through graceful movements. It was then I began to hear the music of my soul's song and with this, a new freedom to soar like a bird as I felt the joy of happiness arise within me.

After a life full of joys, sorrows and disappointments, and many twists and turns, there came a time when I chose to pause and I asked myself

~ what now gives meaning to my life?

It was 1989 and I had just turned forty. This year was to become a pivotal time for me, when I felt called to begin a quest to uncover my true essence at the heart of my being.

I set out as a seeker, knowing only that I felt an urgent need to follow the calling of my heart, unknowingly I was choosing to follow my soul path. Along the way my journey morphed into an adventure that lighted my way, illuminating the unacknowledged feminine energy within me, and through my experiences I awakened to the voice of my Soul.

∽

The story of my journey is told in the *Odyssey of a Creatress* ~ a memoir of my travels to France that became an exploration of the pure, creative essence of the feminine. Below is a brief retelling of my story:

I had visited France many times before but this trip was different, for this time I set out without a clear plan. I was open and trusting and I allowed myself to be guided as my path unfolded before me, often surprising me in unexpected ways. I traveled to a land of mystery, to a place I have always loved. France seems to resonate with my sense of beauty, and there I found myself able to relax into the feminine parts of myself.

I became lost, only to find myself in a place where nature and my inner voice began to speak clearly to me. After three magical days in the villages of Alet les Bains and Quillan I knew my journey had come to an end and it was time to set off for home. I felt blessed, healed and renewed.

Upon my return home, I began to live differently as I listened inwardly for guidance and synchronicities kept appearing before me. I felt a new confidence as I began to risk living creatively in each moment. I was learning to attune myself to an awareness of the pure essence of the Feminine always present within me.

My difficulty came when I found myself unable to express to others the changes I felt deep within. This intensified my belief that I was different and did not fit into the world around me. Feeling invisible and misunderstood I began to look for a language to express my inner truth, to create an intimacy with my soul and to make new meaning for myself. My journey had changed from being an outer seeker to that of an inner seeker, as I looked within to find meaning to the mystery that was my life.

I found myself feeling deprived if I did not read every day, then unfulfilled if I did not write something every day, and so my book began to take shape out of my need for discovery. It took me 22 years to find my voice and to begin writing, thereby gaining a deeper relationship to my personal felt sense of my soul.

The word Creatrix came to me out of a dream –
speaking its meaning to me, saying

***"I am the Creatrix,
The Feminine Essence and counterpart
to the Masculine Creator."***

This energy began to resonate within me, touching into a place in my soul and I felt called to explore the hidden depths of this inner feminine, the 'Yin of my life.'

My writing is guided by the words of the Creatrix, as she shares her wisdom through me. She enters my energy field and she becomes me, or I become her. She speaks through me, most often waking me in the early hours of the morning or at the dawning of the day, with words that arrive fully formed and with flowing grace.

Taking time to listen and to hear her speak her words of wisdom and to consciously welcome her into my life, I honour her intelligence within me. By doing so I have become a Creatress. I find myself standing taller, feeling stronger and becoming clearer, as her intuitive messages flow through me. I feel empowered by the Creatrix within me and I can no longer imagine life without her guidance, for she has become the connector between '*me, my soul and the intelligence of Cosmic Source.*'

I have often wondered about my soul and felt confused as to how it fits into my spiritual journey and so I began to write *The Sacred Dance of Soul* to begin to acknowledge the ancient feminine wisdom within me and discover a way to create my own authentic love story.

I came to know spirit and soul as very different aspects within me. Philosophers of ancient times have long debated over 'what is soul' and kept coming back to the awareness that 'soul' and 'the feminine' are connected. I too have found this to be so. I have spent many years as a seeker of soul, and over time, uncovered feminine mysteries as holding the key to a life of creativity and soul consciousness.

Growing up in the 50's and 60's I learned to be quiet and good and to mistrust my feminine wisdom and I felt my mother's disappointment in her own life as she tried to live vicariously through me. As I began to own my feminine powers, I noticed how this brought fear to the surface in those around me. It challenged the dominance of the patriarchal belief system into which I was born, a world that so often culturally devalued the worth of the feminine perspective.

This mistrust of the feminine and her mystery has meant that many of us carry a wounded sense of self. The link between the intelligence of our body, our heart and the subtle body of our psyche – our heart wisdom and our instinctual knowing – has become disconnected as we favour the cultural dominance of the intelligence of our rational mind.

By disowning our heart wisdom we dishonour our innate Feminine ways of knowing and this creates dis-harmony within. We feel a sense of something missing, an imbalance, on the soul level of our existence.

For many, the idea of listening to the intelligence of our bodies or hearing the lessons our heart is messaging to us, is something we have no time for. Even loving the mystery of life itself, as creativity unfolding and coming into form, is something our scientific hubris will not allow. This dis-ease I refer to as a 'mistrust of mystery,' has led to a loss of inner harmony and a dis-connection towards our personal soul consciousness.

One thing I have learned is that only I can walk my soul path. Others can guide me along the way but it is my inner journey that leads to my empowerment and I know that as you learn to love the truth and beauty of your unique authentic self, you will discover that your life then unfolds before you with ease and grace.

"As soon as you trust yourself, you will know how to live."
~ Johann Wolfgang Von Goethe

INTRODUCTION

The Sacred Dance of Soul is a guide to uncover the feminine intelligence that resides within each and every one of us, with a power that is subtle, magical, mystical and often invisible and yet in our hearts we know it exists.

It is not a 'how to' book but rather a transformational guide to empower you to take the journey into your heart, to know the truth within you and to heal your relationship to the pure creative essence of the feminine; and feel the joy that comes from dancing with your soul with the aliveness of an awakened heart and reclaim the unique beauty of your soul.

PART 1

We introduce you to the pure essence of the Feminine and take a look into the meaning of soul from a feminine perspective, awakening you to her subtle ways of being. Her presence is there to guide you along your path and change the ways in which you make meaning in your life.

PART 2

We enter a transformational journey that awakens our consciousness to the powers within us, as we begin to make new choices that may challenge many of the beliefs we have been taught to place highly among our laws of living.

PART 3

The myth of Persephone is a mother-daughter story. Kore is an innocent maiden who is abducted into the underworld where her experiences become her awakening into her empowered feminine self and her soul consciousness. She enters into the dark mystery realms and upon her return to her mother Demeter, together they create the mystery rites of ancient Greece. We learn from her story, as Queen and partner to Hades and lift the veil on the sacred mystery of soul consciousness.

PART 4

Embracing life as a Creatress means becoming visible and having the courage to express your true self. We experience a re-birth of the Feminine principle, as we expand our perceptions to include an awareness of sacred space, creativity and the wise intelligence of our heart as we step into a new and authentic life story.

PART 5

The Soul's Laws of Living and Languages of Soul, expand upon our awareness of energy consciousness. We reclaim the power of the Great Unconscious, so that we can enrich our lives by including the feminine intelligence of our soul together with cosmic intelligence.

PART 6

We explore the life of a Modern Mystic who is at home with the mystery of both worlds of light and darkness. She has developed her subtle senses, her intuitive and psychic knowing and she is guided by her wise inner feminine soul.

PART 7

We experience an increase in the happiness quotient as a result of fully expressing the creative powers of the feminine within us. Our life becomes art as we re-claim our creativity: the 8 gifts of our Inner Child and Creatress Blessings.

PART 8

Creatress Practices introduces you to some experiential ways to explore and grow into awareness of yourself as a body that is both physical and subtle energy, thereby expanding your conscious and nurturing your soul.

This is followed by Soul therapy and Reminiscing's ~ stories of brief moments in time, of choices made and the smallest of steps taken.

PART I

*By re-valuing the essence of the feminine
We learn new ways of reclaiming the power
Of the feminine in our everyday lives
History, Her-story and a renewal of
The Essence of the Feminine*

1

THE PURE ESSENCE OF THE FEMININE

"Your Soul is the creative essence of the Feminine within you. She knows your truth, at the essential core of your being."

I believe that we are each born with our unique soul story waiting to be lived. For me to express my soul truth has taken many years; to make visible that which has lain buried deep within me waiting to be made conscious. Awakening to soul consciousness means awakening to your feminine wisdom and uncovering the gifts of your authentic self.

You may feel called to explore and discover the soul knowledge of who you are here to become. How to begin is by learning to trust in the ways in which your soul speaks through you, lovingly embracing you just as you are. You know you are far more than your physical body. You have a soul body that carries a memory of ancient feminine wisdom and holds the power to guide you to step into your life as a Creatress and manifest your unique soul story.

The Feminine has been disavowed for centuries and it is time we claimed her worth. Many of us carry shame around owning our feminine power and we hold beliefs that carry distortions of that feminine power, sending it underground, waiting for the time when feminine consciousness can arise renewed.

> Awakening to the voice of your soul is to re-member the feminine ways of living and reclaim the feminine power that is magnetic, magical, transformative and healing.

Are you willing and courageous enough to take this soul journey into the deep mystery of your inner self and to meet with your sacred feminine essence?

If you are, then keep reading because we are about to explore new perspectives on living that expand and ground an understanding of how to value the feminine aspects of yourself and thereby create your own unique life.

This will not only empower you to uncover the truth and beauty that resides at the core of your being but to trust in your soul's wisdom.

Learning to live as a Creatress came out of the writing of *my story* many years after my return home from a trip to the South West of France. My experiences became a catalyst for transformation, as my old life began to unravel. I felt deeply changed within, my perception of subtle energies grew and my sensitivity to my inner world became heightened. After many years of self doubt, I began to write my memoir and I discovered that the Creatrix was guiding me with her words and I felt a growing need to share her words with others.

The Creatrix spoke to me of the heroine's quest, to walk the inner path and to know the invisible mysteries hidden in darkness. Her words have shown me ways to empower myself, giving me the courage to step out of old paradigms; to let go of old stories and to uncover the pure essence of my feminine as soul.

I was finding that to live creatively required me to let go of much of my societal programming and that my ambition for prestige; power and money were no longer motivators. I now held a desire for a simpler life, as I chose to no longer live my life distracted and disempowered by outdated false values.

I began to embody *the Archetype of the Creatrix* within, as I gave myself permission to learn a different way of being. Slowly my trust in my feminine ways of knowing grew stronger and I discovered that my soul's longings expressed through me in many different ways. This is how I began my journey to feminine empowerment.

The Creatrix is the primary fundamentally feminine essence that connects us to the creative forces of nature as they manifest into earthly form. She is that part of you who knows how to trust in your feminine creative powers and be guided by an innate intelligence as it unfolds from within you, in a joyous and loving way.

The Creatrix Speaks ~

"Your Inner relationship with your Wise Soul Self

*Guides you to live a rich life of creative consciousness
Know the soul's laws of living and love all things equally
Let your heart open to the energies of Source and Cosmic Soul."*

Archetypes are constellations of energy across time and space that capture repeating patterns of humankind, naming ways of being that bring meaning to our existence.

The Creatrix manifests as the archetype of the pure Creative Essence of the Feminine, expressing herself with a quality of presence that empowers from within.

She guides me to create my own unique story, and to become the very best expression of my true self that it is possible for me to be as an empowered and unique glowing soul; and to express myself in a way that mirrors the truth and beauty that is within my soul.

By claiming her presence I became a Creatress and I discovered that my soul is inextricably entwined with the loving wise feminine within me. It would take many years of both outer questing and inner searching before I came to know the true meaning of the words below

*"To thy own self be true ...
And it must follow, as the night the day,
Thou canst not then be false to any man."
~ William Shakespeare
Hamlet*

2

BECOMING AN AWAKENED SOUL

Soul awakening brings forth many questions ~ some are full of mystery and others are too big to ever have answers.

Have you ever wondered about your soul?

Have you ever gazed at the first crescent of a new moon low in the early evening sky, just as the sun is setting, and felt a desire to make a wish for something new to begin?

Can you remember a time when you were far away from the city and you looked up at a myriad of stars twinkling in the deep night sky and felt a connection to these stars, too many to ever be able to count, knowing that you belong to them and they to you?

By becoming at one with the stars, this stirs a sparkle within, and a heart connection to *'All that Is.'* These experiences of immense mystery of our miraculous cosmos stir our sense of wonder and childlike innocence and make us feel awakened to our sense of soul, and we feel light and free.

We are living in a time of great change and there is a shift in consciousness taking place. Our souls are calling us to expand into new ways of perceiving and making meaning of our world and our place in it, and to question the values by which we have unconsciously been living our lives.

For centuries the needs of our souls and the ways of the feminine have been shrouded in misconception and often put aside as unworthy of our attention. This has affected the quality of the lives of both men and women, for far too long.

In this fast-paced world full of amazing technology there is a danger that we become our technology or it becomes us. The urge to explain the mysteries of life in scientific terms comes from a need to have intellectual power over our world, to be able to control, manipulate and eliminate the possibility of sacred mystery having any place in our philosophy.

It is now time to lift the veil of negativity and disempowerment towards all that is feminine that centuries of conditioning have laid upon us and to re-evaluate history's stories that encouraged us to fear the powers of the creative feminine. By doing so we begin to re-value the sacred feminine as Herstory, reshaping her worth and reclaiming her powers.

Awakening to soul consciousness means awakening to the feminine wisdom within you and uncovering the gifts of your truth hidden in the shadows of your soul. As you begin to live with an expanded awareness of your self as soul, it becomes natural for you to honour the sacred in the world of nature that surrounds you, and in the everyday patterns of your life.

There are many questions around the subject of soul beginning with:

- What is my soul and where does it come from?
- How can it be found and what does it offer to me?
- How can I create a loving relationship with my soul? These questions lead us into an exploration of soul wisdom.

When you open to hearing the voice of your soul, your heart begins to heal and this connects you to an expanded awareness of yourself as a soul star, a unique expression of cosmic source here on earth.

3

SOUL WISDOM

Your soul is both ancient and very new at the same time and also everlasting. Just as energy merely changes form, so too does your soul. Soul may linger before birth and after death and when it leaves our physical form it returns to the realms of cosmic soul, the home of all memories and imaginings. Soul carries a story that goes back into the past and forward into the future and it is our personal soul that connects us to cosmic soul. It is our bridge between the now and the everlasting realms and our personal connection to the energy of Source.

This other dimension that is Cosmic Soul is where the truth and beauty of each of us is seen, known and recorded forever. This is a world of dark mystery and the dimension of source, home to cosmic soul and universal intelligence that is beyond anything that our limited consciousness can ever conceive.

Your soul knows the truth and beauty that is you, as aliveness within every cell of your being that resonates with your uniqueness. Universal intelligence comes from the energy of

Source, awakening in us an awareness that we are soul expressions, each a Soul Star of cosmic consciousness.

Source is a dimension that is beyond our understanding for it reaches into eternity without the need for the dimensions of time or space. It is infinite essence and home to divine forces that have ineffable powers that manifest into our reality. It vibrates within us in every cell of our being and it is this source energy that carries the power within us to heal. We can briefly touch into the essence of source in numinous moments and feel its presence. It is energy in the purest sense, expressing itself as waves of vibration that exist within everything and throughout all time and space.

We are taught to look outside of ourselves for our answers and yet we hold the key to all we need to know alive within our soul. Soul speaks to us in ways that resonate in our hearts with vibrations of love.

This is not an intellectual exercise that can be rationally explained. Rather it is a whole body experience that includes the emotions and subtle energy fields in and around us. It is as natural as the movement of water that flows and shape shifts over the earth.

Our soul knows our truth and when we let go, relax and trust with an inner focus, guidance comes to us from a source that is far more intelligent than our rational, conscious mind. We are here to become this pure energy of cosmic truth that manifests within us as personal soul and can be felt as the warmth of love in our hearts.

Time spent in communion with our soul is time well spent. When we honour ourselves and all living things including the Earth as the sacred ground of our being, we begin to perceive ourselves as en-souled beings and we glimpse numinous moments of oneness with Cosmic Soul and we find that Sacredness and Soul go together.

There is something about becoming lost, or seemingly losing all, that creates an opening to finding our way back to our soul. This can awaken us to the potential of a life more clearly aligned to feelings of personal empowerment that emerge from letting go of the past and being willing to live in the energy of the moment that connects us to an inner power, that is in service to our soul.

SOUL MESSAGES

Connecting to Soul is a connection to the deep wisdom that guides us to become loving, creative humans. It reveals the knowledge of our gifts and guides us on how to share them with humankind. Our soul resonates with the true essence of our individual uniqueness.

The Creatrix Speaks ~

" It is your soul that guides you when you feel you have lost your way or feel unloved and unlovable. It does so with wisdom that speaks to you through your heart with loving kindness and grace, awakening you to the tune within you that carries the rhythm of your unique song."

Our soul speaks to us through the intelligence of our heart, with vibrations of love and a knowingness that resonates within every cell of our bodies. Each soul has a personal soul story to tell. It is uniquely different for every one of us. The secret is to learn how to hear the music of your soul, singing to you with the innate intelligence in your heart.

Your soul is personal to you alone and it carries the knowledge of your unique story that you are here to create as your personal contribution for the good of all humanity.

You begin to learn the language of your soul when you trust in the ways in which your soul speaks through you with the power of love that embraces your perfect imperfection, accepting you just as you are.

Soul messages come to you in their own time, sometimes when you least expect them. The trick is, to catch these intuitive messages and write them down so that they are not lost. They are like dreams that come to us on the wings of an angel and then are quickly gone. Take time to record your dreams upon waking and any other thoughts that flash into your consciousness when you are in that semi liminal stage between sleep and awaking each morning. Make your soul journal your companion, recording these messages from soul, speaking to you, bringing you precious insights and heart wisdom to guide you along your path.

The voice of your soul speaks directly to you through all your senses, in the language of your body, mind, emotions, imagination and intuitive and psychic knowing. These are all ways of bringing you into alignment with an experience of your reality of authentic wholeness in the present moment – to claim the 'What Is' of your life.

We are energy vibrating in space and time. We know ourselves as physical bodies but we are far more than this. Our body is a vessel we travel in and as such we need to care for our body for it is the sacred container for our soul.

To know your soul deeply is to uncover your essential 'Me' - your personal soul self that transforms the ways in which you make meaning of your life. As you become more sensitive to these messages from your soul you will find you also become more sensitised to the energies of others. Your increased sensitivity requires you to be vigilant of how people and environments affect you. You need to have clear psychic boundaries so that you can make wise choices and protect yourself in ways that honour the voice of your soul, rather than shutting down your sensitivity to yourself and others. This opens the door to the creation of a life of fulfilment as you discover that true empowerment comes from a deep connect to your inner wisdom.

Your soul story is the sacred journey of your heart; becoming conscious of the subtle realms of living and by glimpsing into the Source intelligence of the cosmos and the feminine become your portal to this world of cosmic consciousness.

> *Your awakened Soul shows itself as an inner light that shines, as a sparkle in the eye and as the intensity of the energy of your aura as it glows*

Let the transformational soul journey begin....

PART II

*"The inner story, though the same in essence for all,
Is always single and unique in each human being,
Never before lived and never to be repeated."*

~ Helen Luke

4

CATALYSTS FOR TRANSFORMATION

To walk alone through the darkness of the unknowable path to transformation is to find the way home to your soul, giving you the ultimate power to create an authentic life story for yourself.

We grow up believing that it is our parents, teachers, priests and spiritual guides who know what is best for us and what really matters most in life. Our habit is the practice of looking outside of our selves and placing our trust in others to find answers to many of life's challenges.

While we look to others for all our answers, believing that *'others know better what the best path for me is than my soul does,'* we are choosing not to be guided by the voice of our soul. Yet it is the quality of the relationship we have with our soul which colours all of our inter-relationships with others in the world around us.

Following your soul path is not for the faint hearted. Transformation begins when we change our inner relationship with ourselves and expand our perceptions of the beliefs we hold around the feminine.

First we begin by exploring how fear and doubt can limit us and hold us back from claiming our truth.

As we become conscious of the ways in which we are using our imagination, we learn to listen to our inner thoughts and become aware of the habits we are unconsciously re-creating by the stories we tell ourselves.

So many of these stories are disempowering. They have become so familiar to us that we accept them without question, unconscious of how destructive these repeating messages can be. In this way we are giving ourselves permission to live a life of old habits and repeating patterns that have the power to hold us back from knowing and claiming our truth and of ever being able to step into our unique soul stories.

Often the messages we feed ourselves are there to keep us safe. However unconsciously held beliefs about ourselves can be dangerous and may also be difficult to change, because often we don't know we have them. These voices may have overtones of strict control, using fear to motivate or control and sometimes they may even feel like outright bullying.

By becoming conscious of the disempowering inner stories we tell ourselves; by revealing our fears, doubts and memories, we begin to question these inner stories. This becomes a first step towards releasing us from the power of old negative messages, so they no longer keep us ineffectual, disempowered and small. We can then begin to choose new and empowering stories that change our relationship with ourselves and become catalysts for transformation and real inner change. Then we are able to make new choices and create different outcomes if we should so desire.

Our own inner dialogue can limit our freedom to live our

truth. What needs to change is the way in which we judge ourselves and often deny ourselves permission to follow our dreams, or to hear the truth in our hearts.

There comes a time to wake up and say,

> "Stop, that's enough. I am no longer willing to stay small, for that is not my truth and I am ready to change."

> Ask yourself:
> "Is the story I tell myself, a loving story?"

If you feel disillusioned, disappointed or depressed, it could be time for you to question the very beliefs you build your life upon. Could now be the time to create your own unique soul story, one that expresses the truth and beauty of your soul, as the pure essence of who you are here to become?

- Are you choosing to stay in a reality that you are creating by repeating old habits that no longer serve you well?
- Are you holding on to past memories and reliving them because they are so familiar and you feel as though they keep you safe?
- Are you feeling disempowered from living your life trying to stay in control, appearing to be strong, and underneath fearing the future?
- Are invisible bonds to loyalties from your past keeping you stuck?

THREE HABITS THAT KEEP US REPEATING OLD WAYS OF BEING

We so often feed ourselves with messages based upon

> Worry, Fear and Doubt.

It can feel safer not to question but to maintain the status quo, rather than make waves or upset those around us. By doing so, we keep ourselves essentially unfulfilled as we daily continue to live focused on negative beliefs, limitations and imaginings of *'what if's'* as each day we create our inauthentic lives.

Some may have grown comfortable living from a familiar place of fear-based negativity. They stay stuck in old repeating patterns that do not bring any feelings of creativity or joy and yet they feel they have no other choice.

Worry is something I grew up with as a constant way of being. My mother had been born just after the First World War and became a young adult as the Second World War began. She lived amongst the bombings of London and so understandably she became an expert in worrying. It was as if worrying would protect her or become a catalyst to bring change, none of which was true. Over time I became conscious of my 'worry wart' self, and began questioning the value of this behaviour. I realised that there are far better ways for me to engage with my imagination.

Fear too has a way of controlling us. Our fear of the unknown, of change and the ultimate fear of death, can limit our ability to fully embrace the enjoyment of being alive as creative beings and can hold us back from taking a risk and following the path our soul is calling us towards.

When we doubt and second-guess ourselves, we develop the habit of handing our power over to others, by asking them to choose for us. By doing this we are also choosing to hand over responsibility for our decisions. This means we retain our chance to blame others for our lack of fulfilment. The side effects of this perpetuate feelings of fear and disempowerment and re-confirm our perceived lack of choice over our ability to create our own life story.

When we give our power away to others, we fall into a place of victimhood, and this shows in our energy body for all to see. To collapse into victimhood, feels disempowering. We may choose to place blame onto others for everything we do not like about our lives and in so doing we are also giving our power away to others.

Caroline Myss writes of how we bond with others by connecting through personal stories of our 'woundedness.' By doing so, the danger is that we let our wounds become our identity and our reason for bonds of intimacy and therefore we feel safe as long as we don't change. In this way we may lose our power to heal and grow.

What defines readiness that enables transformational processes to begin?

There comes a time after being absorbed in the experience of endings, loss and grief that we become ready to be kinder and more loving to our self. There can be many times when we may hear the call for transformation and signs that signal its arrival. Feelings of dissatisfaction and depression, often referred to as divine discontent, may act as a catalyst to open the door to experiencing shifts in consciousness that lead us to desire something beyond our everyday life.

Loss can open the door to New Ways of Living

It is part of being human to experience trauma and loss at some time in our lives and the emotions of grief can overwhelm us and make life seem to come to a standstill as we process the loss of something or someone dear to us. This is an experience that none of us gets to escape, as loss is an essential part of life.

Loss of something, or someone dear to you may take you to a place where all meaning and purpose seem to have gone.

Often it is the loss of a dream that we are grieving for, something that never was except in the illusions of our minds; or a search for perfection that failed; and sometimes it is something tangibly real, an accident or an illness that has led us towards experiencing feelings of sadness, anxiety, disappointment and disillusionment.

Grief is so personal and we know within ourselves that we need to take time out, to incubate our hurt self. We know that the past is now gone and life seems to have lost its meaning. We need time to process our experience and time to heal. This grief can rob us of all the joy of living. The place we find ourselves in may force us to step back from our life and go within, and in time we find ourselves entering a place of surrender and the acceptance of 'what is,' knowing that the past will not change.

When we begin to accept our loss, new awareness can shake us awake and become a catalyst for us to search for new meaning. It is then that we begin to look for new answers and this becomes the first step for transformational change.

In this way loss can open the door to new ways of living, including the capacity for greater empathy and compassion and a deeper and more inclusive acceptance of the hidden dimensions and the unacknowledged mysteries of life itself.

As we become ready to release attachment to the past and move towards major change and transformation, there comes a shift in our perspective from outer/ego to inner/soul focus. We begin to make friends with our hidden self and to move towards unknown depths, to reveal the mystery that is buried deep within us. We know when we hear the call that it is time to release the old and begin to create a new life story, one that is in alignment with the journey of our soul.

This journeying we take into the darkness is entering into an unknown territory without a map to guide the way. Often we need to be accompanied by a guide, as in a psychotherapeutic setting, or a close friend who is willing to listen and bear witness to our experiences. This validation by another can help in the often times painful and lonely process of the personal journey of transformation, individuation, and becoming your true and beautiful Soul Star self.

Trauma

The effects of trauma create an experience of shock to the nervous system that can reverberate throughout our lives and affect the everyday choices we make without our being aware of the power that these memories stored in our cells have over us. Abuse sends messages to our brain that are negative and damaging and again we may not be aware of the effect these have upon our lives. Yet we can feel powerless to change the repeating patterns of our lives, when the autonomic thoughts and core messages we are living by exist without our conscious awareness of them.

Depression to me, is a sign of soul sickness. When depression descends upon us, it can present us with a questioning of meaning that sends us into dark places where all seems lost and we meet with our fears that may be connected to past life memories, familial history or personal experiences of trauma. The task becomes to face our fears and choose to release their hold over us. We can make space within for something new to arise by relaxing into becoming honest, real and true to ourselves.

Emotions are energy in motion that I liken to the movement of waves arising up out of the ocean. Emotions rise up to be felt and then fall back to join the great ocean of unconsciousness again. When we lock onto the emotion of the wave, unwilling to let it go, we become one with it and allow it to pull us down into the ocean's depths. By doing so we can find ourselves falling into our familiar disempowering patterning of depression, sadness, anxiety or fear.

We need to catch ourselves as we find ourselves falling below the surface, and take a pause, create a space and ask ourselves.

> *"Do I want to lose myself in a low energy state of disempowerment or do I have the courage to choose to step outside of this old patterning and create a different and more satisfying experience?"*

To be able to take the choice to reflect upon our experience, to become conscious of the energy flowing within us and to let this emotional energy pass through us like waves upon the ocean as they morph naturally into other forms, is a very freeing experience.

TRANSITION AND BEYOND - INTO THE SHADOW LANDS

There are many opportunities to embark on a journey of deep inner change and to thereby open our selves to a sense of the sacred in our everyday lives. When we enter the grey world of depression, we find ourselves caught in the Shadow Lands, an in-between world of lightness and darkness. It is a place where the known and the unknowable meet in a place that so often carries with it confusion, pain and suffering. This is the place where we come face to face with our demons that hold us to ransom and we find ourselves trapped in a loveless world full of doubts and imaginary fears. Our perceptions are distorted. We need to take time to acknowledge the emotional content of any traumas that have shaped our life until now, and by doing so, to free us to experience a deeper and expanded connection with our unconsciousness made conscious.

When we find ourselves living in the Shadow Lands, we are no longer fully present to ourselves or to the world around us. Colour is missing from our lives as we dress in grey and dream in black and white and passion is no longer present in our lives. There is no time for play or laughter of any kind, and all seems to be lost. This is a place of grief and pain that leaves us feeling depleted and deeply tired and robs us of our joy. Any real change requires us to be willing to let go of old memories and habits that no longer work for us and to take time to feel into our buried truth, whatever that may be.

When we begin to question the beliefs we live by that may no longer be serving us well and the illusion of permanence that we are holding on to, we become more aware of unconscious habits that have been holding us in our repeating patterns of behaviour. This can have the effect of stirring up an instinctual fear of change. Letting go of this fear can place us more closely in contact with deep sadness beneath this fear and to the pain that lives in our heart. When we do this, we can sometimes feel isolated and alone as we experience the dark night of the soul. If you find yourself here know that you don't need to do this alone.

Part of becoming empowered is to be able to reach out, be receptive and share with trusted others. When we allow our painful emotions to be felt we open ourselves to all the pain we have been carrying in our hearts. This brings to the surface messages from within that communicate the longings of our soul.

We don't have to do it all alone
Being present in the moment
Trusting our inner knowing
And our connection to Source
Allows life's creative process to unfold

Practical and magical mysteries combine
And we become more than we ever
Imagined our selves to be

It is true that the darkest night is always followed by a new moon that symbolises a time when something new can begin to take shape. A mentor or guide can help by holding an image of our highest potential as we take baby steps towards letting go of our old self and transitioning into a life of expanded consciousness by re-connecting to the essential core essence of our being.

This requires letting go of the fear projected on to the mysteries of life and being willing to enter the dark womb of life, a space out of which all new life emerges; the ultimate place of creation of all humankind. This also means accepting that movement and change are a natural part of the cycles of life.

It is possible that much of the illness we experience comes from blocked or stagnant 'chi' energy. Our fears and unconscious patterns that hold us in repeating patterns of behaviour can originate from emotional issues from our past, toxic experiences and environments, and disempowering social norms. Change can only come from within each of us as we decide not to accept the status quo; we then become willing to navigate the path of change. This is when transformation becomes the act of dying to your old self, so you can discover that which is authentic and true for you.

WAYS TO FOSTER PERSONAL SOUL CONSCIOUSNESS

When happenings trigger a crisis in our lives, this has the potential to become a catalyst for transformation, opening us to new levels of perceptions of a wise intelligence present within us all. It is this 'Me' that we are longing to know and have an intimate relationship with, so that we can blossom and grow to fulfil the promise of our soul's potential.

Taking back our projections and owning our shadow are a necessary part of this individuation process. Facing the unknown, going into the darkness and meeting our shadow self, allows us to mature into a more inclusive, forgiving and authentic life.

Become a chooser. It is not that you don't listen to others to hear their perspectives or consider all your options as you explore known possibilities, but as the chooser, you become willing to be responsible for the outcomes of your own choices. Observe how you are using your imagination and ask yourself:

> "Is this feeding negativity by instigating images of the worst possible outcome or constantly recalling the least desirable memory?"

If you are using your imagination to focus in this way then you are doing yourself a great disservice. When daring to step outside of your self-defeating old patterns, you need to stop and consider. Go within and ask yourself,

> "Does this reality feel true for me and if not, dare I live by a different reality, one that is guided by the inner wisdom of my essential self?"

Trust in yourself only comes when you are willing to take one small step in the direction of your dreams, allowing your path to unfold before you as you trust that the outcome will reveal itself in its own time. Claiming clear boundaries is a necessary step to overcome old patterns of fear. This means letting others clearly know what you say yes or no to so your inner trust can begin to grow.

Courage comes to the fore as you begin to move in the direction of your unique path allowing it to creatively unfold before you.

"Creativity takes courage" ~ Henri Matisse

It takes courage to step out of old paradigms and let go of old stories. Often those around us are vested in our staying the same as before. Change can be a scary prospect for our selves and for others. It can feel much safer to not rock the boat and to keep the status quo. The need to not make waves, or upset others, may keep us from living our truth.

You will only hear the whispers of your soul calling you when you take time to step outside of the busyness (business) of your life, to relax and be willing to sit quietly with yourself and to listen. Until you take time out to be with yourself, you will miss the soul's subtle wisdom and devalue the feminine essence within you. Not only hearing these messages but making the stories we tell ourselves into permission-giving messages makes it easier to open to our creative feminine soul.

Ask yourself ~
"Are you extending your generosity to yourself or are you a hard taskmaster or a workaholic, believing that doing is the only way to justify yourself in the world, finding it difficult to allow yourself the time to be quiet and relaxed, open to listen and to dream, and be caring and kind to yourself?"

NEW CHOICES AND TRUTH THAT SETS YOU FREE

To make new choices first requires that we undo the many habits that keep us living our lives on automatic pilot, repeating these old patterns. Awareness becomes the first step to awakening real change and new perspectives that arise become catalysts for our transformation. Real change begins with a shift within oneself and healing happens from the inside outward, just as inner focus motivates outer actions.

Your soul requires simplicity and honesty in your relationship with your Self. When you become congruent with your hidden inner depths and uncover your truth, you become an awakened soul. As you begin to nurture and love yourself with quiet kindness, your soul intensifies into an inner glow that shines out of the darkness in a way that can be seen and felt by others.

Is happiness something you can dare to claim for yourself?

By this I mean a happiness that arises spontaneously from within you for no particular reason at all. As your heart opens and your sensitivity to energy becomes heightened, you will feel a well of inner joy, warmth in your heart and a golden glow from your soul.

Having the courage to follow your heart and trust in your inner wisdom is giving yourself permission to live from your authentic 'Me.' Your soul becomes your very best friend, constantly there, always kind and loving, and totally wise.

Failure is an option. The greatest learning may come from our failures. They guide us to learn and grow and redirect our energy elsewhere, gracefully guiding us to recognise our unique and authentic path in life.

Warning: once you are awakened to the wisdom of your soul and have chosen to follow this path, there can be no turning back or returning to the old you. You will feel a truth in your body, your heart and in your bones that resonates from deep within, awakening your creativity and passion for living. Following a new path, with rules that are different to those you have been taught in the past, means owning your power to create and manifest a new story.

As we reclaim our feminine wisdom, so our soul energy grows. We raise our vibrations to include the subtle energies of our psyche. This sends waves of energy into the world, vibrating in tune with the quality of the energy we carry within us.

As the desire to live creatively grows and we find ourselves being called to activate the artist within us, and the small and simple things of life begin to matter.

It's all an inside job ~
Healing, loving, creating and being, all come from a maturing connection to our inner life and an expanded consciousness that we as human beings are expressions of source energy, as soul in this moment of time.

Now we will explore Persephone's journey into the darkness of the underworld ~

The natural world knows and trusts itself and it has a beauty and simplicity that is intelligence, that emanates out of lightness and darkness

PART III

*"The true light never hides the darkness but is born out
Of the very centre of it, transforming and redeeming
So to the darkness we must return, each of us individually
Accepting his ignorance and loneliness, his sin and weakness
And most difficult of all consenting to wait in the dark
And even to love the waiting"*

~ Helen M Luke

5

THE MYTH OF PERSEPHONE

The Myth of Persephone and Demeter is an archetypal daughter/mother story of loss and empowerment that begins with Persephone's abduction into the mystery realms of the underworld. This is said to be the myth describing the creation of the seasons but I have found its meaning reaches beyond, into an awareness of sacred mysteries.

In *The Odyssey of a Creatress* I explored the myth of Psyche (meaning *soul*) as a journey to finding true love (Eros) that begins with learning the love of self. Psyche shone her lamp to light up the truth that lies hidden within each of us, so that the real you beneath the surface can be seen and known. She was challenged by lessons set by Aphrodite and she uncovered the feminine path to know her self; trust in and love herself for who she truly was, and to finally re-unite with Eros.

These myths help us to understand something that needs to be experienced to be fully understood. Your soul journey is a knowing that is not easy to put into words.

The myths of Persephone and Psyche are about beautiful feminine beings who awaken us to the sacred feminine as the pathway to soul; with Psyche ~ butterfly/soul and Persephone ~ the guide of souls in the Underworld.

Kore's Story (as daughter)

The myth begins with an innocent young maiden, daughter of Demeter and Zeus, out with her friends in the fields enjoying the sunshine and the spring flowers. Her mother, the Goddess of the Harvest, adores her beautiful young daughter and has always protected her innocence and kept her safe.

Until this time, Kore (meaning maiden) has gone along with her life without question and is seemingly happy; but a curiosity has begun to awaken in her and she feels a desire to spread her wings and venture further afield. Her curiosity is piqued as she spies an unusual flower. As she reaches out to pick this beautiful narcissus flower, the earth suddenly opens up and Hades (God of the Underworld) in his horse drawn carriage claims Kore, sweeping her into his arms carrying her into the depths of the Underworld. Within seconds she is gone and by the time Demeter discovers Kore is missing, there is no trace of her to be found anywhere.

Only Hecate, the old Goddess of the dark moon and the crossroads, hears Kore cry out as she is carried away into the darkness. What Demeter and Kore do not know is that this abduction is the working of two great gods, the brothers Zeus and Hades. Zeus as Kore's father has contracted with his brother Hades for his daughter to become Hades' bride, the deed arranged without any discussion with mother or daughter.

Hades, the God of the Underworld was in love with beautiful Kore and Zeus knew that Demeter would not agree to the union. And so on the day of her fateful abduction, as Kore stepped outside of her usual world in search of something beautiful and different, the earth opened up before her and she was taken into the depths of the underworld. All she knows is that Hades swept her up in his arms and the earth closed over her. The narcissus flower is no more and she finds herself in a dark and mysterious, unknown world.

This experience is a total shock for Kore; a mystery and great loss for her mother Demeter – but totally expected by her father Zeus and Hades, who has claimed his bride.

Kore had always seemed a little otherworldly, slightly fey, with an affinity for nature and an ability to observe the energy of a person rather than the words they spoke. She carried the innocence and beauty of a young maiden and wanted to please her mother who was a powerful presence in her life. Her story quickly changed however as she finds herself with Hades in the darkness of the Underworld, catapulted into a dramatic transition and an awakening of her womanhood. Her story now goes very quiet and we do not hear anything from, or about Kore, for some time to come.

Demeter's Story (as mother)

What we do know is that Demeter is deeply wounded by this happening and is overwhelmed by feelings of loss and heartfelt pain. She leaves her temple and wanders the land in search of any clue to her daughter's whereabouts. As time passes with no news of her daughter, Demeter falls into a state of deep depression. She no longer cares about her duties as the Goddess of nature and all growing things. Demeter has entered a transition zone where she experiences the depth of her loss and finds herself feeling both fearful and alone, and the land around her begins to reflect her inner world. The plants stop growing and begin to wither and die, the landscape becomes barren and empty, and famine ravages the land.

As she wanders the earth, she no longer looks like the Goddess she is, but rather a disheveled old woman. After some time she is welcomed into a castle where she takes some rest and is soon offered the task of taking care of the Queen's baby. At last she has found something meaningful to do. Being an immortal goddess she takes the baby and holds it over the fire every evening so that it too will become immortal. One evening the Queen enters the room and sees this happening. Overcome with fear she seizes her baby from Demeter, who is banished from the queen's rooms and stays in the background in the castle.

Some time later, she watches as Baubo, an old servant woman, performs her suggestive antics of silly, outrageous fun and she finds herself laughing out loud, the kind of belly laugh that takes over the whole body. This awakens in Demeter memories of a forgotten past and an experience of happiness, if only for a few minutes. Demeter now declares to the Queen the truth of who she is and reclaims her place as the Goddess of the Harvest. She asks for a Temple to be built in her honour in this city called Eleusius.

Demeter then returns home to seek answers to the mystery of her daughter's disappearance. Hecate, hearing of her return, goes to tell Demeter all she has learned of the part that Zeus had played in the mysterious disappearance of her daughter.

By this time Zeus has become anxious, realising the impact his decision has had upon Demeter and his people, who are now suffering from the ensuing famine. He needs Demeter to restore fertility and growth to the land and so he meets with her to negotiate a solution. Zeus wants to keep his brother Hades happy, as well as come to an agreement with Demeter and so he agrees to Kore's return from the Underworld, on one condition, that if she has eaten of the fruits of the underworld, she must return there.

THE RETURN OF KORE TO THE UPPER WORLD

Over the time that Kore was missing, Demeter felt a lost connection to the world of nature and to her own heart. It was as if her heart was broken open and all she could feel was the pain of her loss. Upon her daughter's return she realises that Kore is no longer the innocent maiden of her memories, with flowers in her hair, who looks to her mother for guidance and protection.

The renewed relationship between Mother and Daughter is no longer the same. Kore has returned to the world of her childhood a confident, mature and empowered Queen in her own right. She has gained confidence as a woman and her partnership with Hades has been fulfilling for her. To become the daughter again without also being his Queen is not her wish. Although she is pleased to see her mother again, she does not appear overjoyed at being rescued.

She surprises her mother with the maturity she has gained. Her arranged marriage to Hades appears to have turned out well. Kore is taller now and she stands proud and strong with an inner light that shines all around her. She now has the new name of Persephone, which means

"She who shines in the dark."

Demeter soon discovers that Persephone has eaten pomegranate seeds while in the underworld, and thus, in accordance with the pact with Zeus, she must return again to this other realm. And so it is, that in spring and summer Persephone returns to Demeter and everything becomes fertile, the crops grow abundantly and there is rejoicing for the new growth that is restored to the land. Then as autumn and winter follow, Persephone returns to her role as Queen in the Underworld and the land becomes fallow.

This myth of the creation of the seasons honours the cycles of death and rebirth; and is where Persephone's story often ends.

PERSEPHONE – AN EMPOWERED WOMAN

Persephone has journeyed into the underworld and returned alive and well and during her time there, she has become a mature and creative woman and she has blossomed into her womanhood. Her new role as Queen of the Underworld, places her in a domain where darkness becomes her friend and magic and mystery abound. She learns to see with different eyes and to appreciate the nature of energy in its many different and subtle forms.

> She has uncovered her power as a woman who is valued, respected and loved for who she is.

> She owns her sexuality as a natural part of the magnetic powers of her feminine creativity.

> She is at home in this Other World; she guides lost souls on their way home to cosmic soul.

> Persephone knows the laws of the underworld, where darkness has its own light and real beauty can be seen as the core essence within every soul.

She has become an empowered Goddess, comfortable in the feminine ways of knowing and being. She has learned to listen within and be guided by the voice of her soul, finding her way in this other world of darkness, instincts and mystery. She has glimpsed into the mysteries of all creation

Persephone has the privilege to see into the depths of another's soul and like the Black Virgin she can see the essence of the beauty in others as she protects and guides them to enter a place of pure love, leaving all their pain and fear behind.

> Just as some Black Virgin Statues are kept below ground in the crypts of churches, the most famous being *La Vierge Noire sous la terre*, locked away in the underground crypt at Chartres Cathedral in France. Persephone too lived in the underworld ~ sous la terre ~ the inner world of soul consciousness

Persephone and the Black Madonna are both archetypal expressions of an ancient primal force of the great mother. She is mystery unfolding out of darkness, feminine creative essence and protector to souls rebirthing out of or transitioning back to cosmic soul.

> She is the protector of orphans and outcasts and anyone who has lost their way. She is powerful and wise and is always there to assist a soul in need with her loving kindness.

The French call the Black Madonna, *La Vierge Noire*. She is our light in the darkness, our compass when we are lost and our experience of wisdom that is the truth that lives hidden within us. In Częstochowa, a city in Southern Poland the Black Madonna is known as Our Lady of Częstochowa and is revered as both Queen and protector of Poland.

Persephone knows that her soul speaks through the whole of her in many subtle ways. She has developed empathy and sensitivity, and has become self-possessed, gracious and empowered in this other realm where she accompanies souls in transition with loving kindness and care. She glows in the darkness, becoming a beacon of light for souls to follow.

Persephone made a pivotal choice by eating some seeds of the pomegranate before returning to her mother. This conscious act became the first step in choosing for her self, and had far reaching consequences for her mother, Demeter and her world.

For Persephone to be deeply loved, to be fully present to her own sexuality and able to stand in her own power, suggests Hades has fostered her becoming an empowered feminine queen of her domain. Demeter realises that there must have been mutual love, respect and intimacy between her daughter and Hades.

Hades is a mature and masculine King, secure in the knowledge of his powers, and open to appreciation of the creative powers of the feminine (for he knows them within himself.) He was ready to welcome his Queen beside him as his equal. He appreciates Persephone's innocence and values her beauty and grace. He knows that if he wants Persephone to be his loving bride and Queen at his side, he needs to treat her with honour and respect; and that if he loves her well, she will blossom into the mature woman he hopes to have as his wife. And so he gives her time to acclimatise to her new surroundings, knowing that she is experiencing a shock as she awakens to a dark and mysterious world.

I believe that if Persephone had been bullied, dominated or raped, she would not have freely chosen to eat the food of the underworld, ensuring her return as Queen of her dark realm and cementing her partnership to Hades. She is now his feminine counterpart and side-by-side they rule their mysterious realm. Her domain is the bridge between our world and the world of cosmic intelligence. She has learned to gracefully transition between being present as a living soul on earth and her role as Queen of the Underworld.

Persephone has been introduced to her sensuality in the underworld. She has chosen to embrace the mysteries of this other realm and has been able to digest her experiences in this place of darkness. She has met her fears and explored her depths as she senses her way and uncovers the riches buried there. She understands the value of time and space for incubation as a pre-condition for all creativity, from formlessness into form and back again.

Some versions of her story describe her as pregnant on her return to the upper world. This can be interpreted as a symbol of her sexuality, fertility, creativity and the bringer of new life; the outcome of her union with Hades and a reason for celebration at the re-uniting of daughter, mother, and potentially grandmother.

Persephone has become a wisdom keeper aligned to the unfolding creativity and rebirth of nature that personifies the essence of the empowered Feminine, in touch with her inner soul. She has been transformed from Kore the maiden into Persephone the Queen, shining her light in darkness and has embraced her role as guide to souls in transition.

Hecate, the Goddess of the Crossroads, helped Demeter uncover the mystery of her daughter's disappearance. She is also there to guide us at times of transition and choices. She is said to have taken Persephone's place in the underworld in spring and summer when Persephone is with her mother, so dead souls in transition were never abandoned.

What is mystery but that which cannot be explained by rational analysis? We do however have experiences that touch us with numinous moments of magic that make the presence of mystery known to us. As women who long to make their way in the outer world, many of us have forgotten the feminine art of how to be receptive and to let go and flow gracefully with the dance of our soul. Entering the feminine state of receptivity opens us to new possibilities and to universal intelligence.

Hermes, the messenger God was sent to retrieve Persephone from the Underworld. Like him she is now able to move between these two worlds of the physical and the numinous dimensions of soul consciousness. She has become a shape shifter and an alchemical guide for souls entering the transition phase between life and death. She straddles the space between our known world and the dimension of cosmic soul.

Some call Persephone the Queen of the dead and think of the Underworld as Hell. And letting go into the darkness of the unknown can feel like going into a fearful void; yet it is a realm full of rich potentiality and home to the creative processes of transitions, of birth, death and rebirth, and the way into a connection to the cosmic intelligence of Source.

Persephone's path shows how to connect to our deeper authentic self and learn to trust the creative process ~ that something new is emerging.

THE ANCIENT ELEUSINIAN MYSTERY RITES

Entering the Mysterium ~ a place of dark mystery. This story is about the maturing of a mother/daughter relationship where together Demeter and Persephone combined their powers and knowledge to become Creatresses of the Eleusinian Mystery Rites.

Persephone and Demeter both spent time waiting in the darkness of not knowing and entered an inner journey where they died to their old selves before they could be reunited, each with their unique gifts. They are Goddesses who know how to honour creativity, growth and cycles of death and rebirth and to navigate the transition zone of mystery between life and death.

Demeter's wisdom is of the natural cycles of all living things in the upper world of physicality and form, from conception, birth, and flowering into fullness, to letting go and releasing form/matter back into the earth.

Persephone's wisdom is her knowledge of the two worlds ~ the physical world of her mother and the world of Hades, King of the alchemical zone of darkness where life meets death; with the task of protectress of souls transitioning back to the unknowable realm of Cosmic Soul; An expansive domain that embraces freedom that is far more than we are able to imagine.

Demeter and Persephone held the Mystery Rites annually at the Eleusinian Temple, giving others an experience of the Alchemical magic and mystery of these secret rites. They taught emotional and social intelligence through a sequence of experiences involving rituals of bathing, sacrificing and dancing, followed by journeying, dreaming and the experience of a symbolic descent into the Underworld.

We do not know the details of the initiatory processes known as the Eleusinian Rites, for they were held in secret, retaining their dark mystery. We do know that those who undertook this experience and faced their fear of death returned to their lives changed at a fundamental level. With the freedom to be true to themselves, to see others as equals no matter their circumstances, they lived by a different set of values, ones that resonated with the calling of their souls.

These secret rites are thought to have included experiences of disorientation, incubation, death/regeneration, leading to an ascent/rebirth, followed by celebrations. They provided a place in which to experience depth and intimacy with your self in preparation for rebirth into a life of soul conscious, learning to value self as soul and understand death as part of the eternal cycle of the rebirth of souls.

These mystery rites guided initiates to face their imaginary fears and to question the beliefs that created the foundation of their lives, thereby uncovering simple truths. Through these experiential rituals that honour the timeless principles of the regeneration of life, they guide seekers into the deeper mysteries and the secrets to happiness, by initiating them along the feminine path and into a life of soul consciousness.

The outcome manifests as happiness, laughter, singing and dancing; a felt sense of fulfilment and freedom and lightness of being; and a desire for the celebration of the pure joy of living.

PERSEPHONE – GREEK MYTH – MODERN MYSTIC

Persephone has become empowered from within and the light of her soul shines brightly in her seemingly dark domain. She is able to move freely between both worlds and possesses knowledge of dark mysteries and wisdom that comes from soul consciousness. She does not fear the darkness and she has met with the depths of her soul and uncovered her true feminine essence hidden there.

Like a cat she sees clearly in the darkness and she has the privilege to see into the depths of another's soul. She sees the essence of their beauty and guides them to enter a place of pure love, leaving all of their pain and fear behind. She has become the midwife of souls as they transition between the physical and cosmic realms and she represents spring and rebirth of new life.

Becoming a Persephone woman means knowing the powers of Alchemy and being able to live in two worlds.

Gods of ancient times were immortal beings with the power to shape shift. Persephone has learned how to shape shift, to move between the two worlds, to walk in another's shoes and to feel as they feel, bringing qualities of empathy and intimacy to her relationships.

She knows your soul as the eternal part of you that is able to shape shift, pre-birth and post-birth and to join with cosmic soul.

Here is a quote I found in *Persephone Rising* that describes beautifully the essence of the mature Persephone.

> *"Persephone not as victim, a woman on a quest of sexual depth and power transcending the role of daughter, though ultimately returning to it as an awakened Queen."*
> Suzanne Banay Santo ~ *Persephone Under the Earth*

The Persephone woman has an expanded sense of awareness of space and time. She travels into the darkness and the mystery of the unknowable realms and has gained knowledge of the secret rites of regeneration. She knows that creativity is the core essence of her being. She trusts in her intuition as inner knowing, she flows with energy that is e-motion and feels into her heart with an energy of unbounded love.

As you begin to value a life of simplicity and truth you will discover that life becomes a dance that meanders like a river with movements of grace and flow. By living this way, you connect with the core essence of feminine creativity and vibrate with the energy that is the music of your soul, as you dance in a river of love.

Courage is necessary if we are to claim our feminine power – and it begins with being able to hold a space for the creative possibility of miracles. In this space qualities are gained of innocence, openness, equableness and honesty, as the simple and spontaneous expressions of the pure essence of self.

This path is often mysterious and can take you on a circuitous route, offering experiences that allow you to grow and learn more about yourself, others and the world.

A sure sign that you are living in alignment with your soul is when you experience happiness arising from within you for no particular reason except for the joy of living a life of truth and authenticity.

> To be a mature Persephone woman is to become a Modern Mystic, with an expanded consciousness that is both inner and outer focused ~ dipping into this inner world of mystery as well as living in the outer world of physical form, grounded and connected to the Earth and to the Cosmos.

Persephone's archetypal journey is as valid today as it was in the times of the mystery schools of ancient Greece. Each person's journey into the underworld is uniquely their own. Each contains the essential elements of facing fears, integrating the shadow and owning the gifts of pure essence; uncovering the core truth that is contained within their soul.

Persephone's story is a classic tale ~ of her experiences in the realms of darkness and the sacred mysteries
~ from innocent maiden to the ways of the mystic

PART IV

Then Sunrise kissed my Chrysalis
~ And I stood up~ and lived ~

~ Emily Dickinson

BECOMING VISIBLE, STEPPING INTO A NEW STORY

*A Creatress trusts in her creative powers
as she matures into her empowerment.
She knows that source is within her, and
Creativity is the raison d'être of her soul.*

The feminine and soul are inextricably entwined, the one reflects the other and they are about our relationship to creativity at the core of our being. When we include the feminine perspective, we cannot help but see our lives as sacred expressions of our soul. This sense of the sacred is within everything and every time we devalue our feminine essence, we also devalue our soul. This not only affects our relationship with others but even more importantly the relationship we have with ourselves.

Ask yourself, "is my inner self talk loving, kind and empowering to me?"

Your 'yes' to this question is a true sign that you have a loving relationship with yourself. Love is the greatest force on earth, an energy that resonates in the heart with an intelligence that connects us all and activates the creative essence within the soul.

There is a simplicity and grace to living as a Creatress that throws our unconsciously held beliefs around power into question. As you reach down and touch the very young child within and awaken to that sense of wonder of the beauty and magic that is all around you, life takes on a different quality and experiences of happiness become a natural part of your everyday living.

Einstein knew this curious inner child self. He also knew the power of sitting with a question, holding a space open and waiting for inspiration to come to him in its own time and he was conscious enough to know how to catch it when it arrived and to hold on to it long enough to bring it into form. New ideas, new perspectives, innovations and answers are there, floating in the etheric realms of our universe waiting to be received by us and made manifest on our human plane of existence.

You can develop a new relationship with the feminine when you make friends with your soul. You don't need a Shaman, Alchemist or High Priest of Priestess to mediate for you to know your soul. That is a belief I have come to question, for I believe that we have been conned with the idea that the answers we seek are outside of ourselves. Not only is this disempowering, it is also profoundly untrue.

Mentors and guides can assist by creating a safe container to explore your awareness of yourself as a complex mix of energies and to guide you as you travel into other states of consciousness. Thereby connecting you to experiences that are ineffable, numinous mystery, and changing your perceptions of yourself, your world and the cosmos. The aim is for these experiences to ultimately lead you to develop a deeper trust and belief in your ability to sense and trust in the more subtle realms of intelligence within you and strengthen your sense of positive self-regard.

There are shifts in your perceptions that when made expand your understanding of yourself and your world, from an eagle's perspective. Your conscious perspective of your life is changed; your values, your habits and everyday rituals change too, as you begin to follow the wisdom of your soul.

Questions begin to arise:

Do I want to stay in this repeating reality that I create by holding on to old memories, or do I desire a new reality and have I the power to create one?

Do I dare to be different, to step out of the old patterning and to go beyond the expectations of self and others; to risk becoming the master of my ship and the Creatress of my reality?

Do I choose to use my time focused on doubts and fears or do I use my imagination wisely to lift my energy and feed my dreams?

REBIRTH OF THE FEMININE

To live an authentic life means to be willing to take a risk, make a change and step into a new reality, a life of your own choosing. There are new psychic muscles to be strengthened and consciousness to be expanded to include a perspective that honours magic, and creativity as essential aspects of your life as sacred mystery.

As you become aligned with a 'soul way' of living, you will find that there is no going back. The old you is gone and the only way forward is to face the unknowable path unfolding before you that leads to a rebirth of the essential truth of who you are here to become. The chrysalis has broken open and it is no longer possible to return to your past self. This is the nature of transformation and why it is so very powerful. In time you will notice that the world begins to reward you for your courage and for owning your inner changes that have been hard won. You have to be brave to follow your own inner knowing, but after a while it feels like you no longer have a choice, even though this may go against most of what you have previously been taught.

Just as the lion's task was to find his courage/heart in the story of Wizard of Oz. Courage is needed to provide the time, space and inner freedom to create your new soul story. As you begin along this creative path, you will meet the fear of vulnerability that arises in you and you may begin to question and second-guess yourself. Notice the feelings that arise and ask yourself ~

Are they valid in my life today
and are they serving my highest good
or are they keeping me small?

It is our relationship with ourselves that sets the tone for all of the outer relationships we have with others. We teach those around us how to treat us by the way in which we treat ourselves. The challenge then remains to develop a strong connection to all that is Feminine in all her physical, emotional and intuitively soulful ways.

She communicates to us with subtle messages without the need for doing or speaking ~ messages we ignore at our peril. Through experiential learning over time, it is possible to move from mistrust to a deeply felt trust in her wisdom ways.

To give yourself a quiet space, a sanctuary where you can listen inwardly, can be the most valuable thing you do for yourself every day. This can be a small corner of a room; a space created by a circle of trees in a forest; sitting with your back resting against a tree, or on the rocks beside the ocean listening to the waves, with the sun on your face and the sand beneath your feet. (These are some of my favourite spaces to just be.)

Developing this relationship to our soul can be transformational and healing as we connect to a loving wisdom within us, which ultimately leads us into our maturity as we embody the loving presence of the Creatress. A Creatress who is simplicity and honesty and connected to her personal power.

This is not the self-love of a narcissist who loves them self in a self aggrandising way that is self absorbed and unable to empathise with the needs or feeling of others. These souls carry a need to have power over others and often their behaviours are driven by fear and lack, not the inclusiveness of love.

It can help to be guided by those who have already walked the path of soul consciousness and learned rituals and practices that assist in raising insight, inspiration and awareness to the sacred and wise intelligence within.

As you learn to trust your unfolding path you will experience guidance in unexpected ways and your ability to manifest becomes effortless as synchronicity, prophetic dreams and crystal clear intuitions guide you.

Your soul path will gracefully guide you on what seems a meandering path towards the lessons and experiences that help you to become strong and true. Then you will not come to the end of this physical life saying, ' I wish I had followed my heart and lived the life my soul desired.'

To go beyond the known requires that you allow a deep and real relationship to grow with the feminine within you. Take notice of your feelings and love your body as a sacred vessel for your soul. To do so you make friends with your heart that links the inter-relational intelligence of mind, body and soul.

> *"Soul awareness grows when you allow yourself*
> *Time to sit in silence and commune with your soul*
> *And feel her love for you, just the way you are.*
> *Her guidance is there to help you to flow*
> *Gracefully in the dance of your life."*

PREPARING THE GROUND FOR A NEW SOUL LIFE

Preparation for the transformational journey of stepping into your authentic soul story has required you to let go of the repeating old stories and old identities and step outside of your known world, to gain another perspective on your life. The task before you is to become conscious of your old patterns of reactive behaviour, to begin to change your relationship to these habits of the past and to know you can make new choices. Be willing to move forward, just one step at a time and trust in your energy's flow and join with the river of your life, as it gracefully unfolds before you.

When we respect ourselves, this sense of connection to our inner power gives us the ability to show others how we wish to be treated. When you shower yourself with positive self-regard and empathy towards your imperfect self, this is a form of self-respect that becomes a true expression of self-love.

Soul guidance comes with tiny hints that when followed, lead us to take one small step, then another in the direction of our dreams, letting go of having to know the outcome.

This is the principle of becoming that is the core essence of the feminine, which requires the trust and courage needed to risk stepping out in a new direction and allowing the path to reveal itself over time. When we have the courage to act, the smallest action can lead to an amazing outcome.

As momentum builds, you find that your heart is with you on your journey. Thank others for their opinions but only follow that which feels deeply true for you.

Take notice of how you are using your imagination and focus on emotions that feed your vision and then enjoy becoming a Creatress as your path unfolds before you.

Does your heart sing and do you feel the joy of being authentically '*You*'?

A soul life requires a life of courage and believing in yourself, that leads to freedom, with a truth and beauty all is own.

Your soul resonates in every corner of your being and speaks your true nature as you move from busyness to presence.

> *When you give yourself permission to explore and play,*
> *Your curiosity sends your fear away.*

MAGNETISM AND CREATIVITY

Creativity begins behind the scenes in darkness. It is fed by imagination and needs space and time to evolve and grow in its own special way. In time we learn to sit in darkness and love the waiting there, for it is this place where we can tap into the fertile richness of potentiality that precedes any creation of new form.

The underworld is a place where souls commune with the unspoken mysteries of life. Soul carries a different set of values and is open and receptive to secrets that are hidden in the darkness and to the expressions of your inner gifts.

That which you focus on becomes you, creating an energy force where like attracts like. It is the feminine magnetic energy of your soul which when activated becomes a golden glow and you find yourself experiencing synchronistic happenings that affirm you are on your true soul path.

The soul's path may seem to meander without a clearly defined direction, and lead you along an unexpected path and yet it can reveal surprising outcomes at times along the way. It can lead you to experiences that make your heart sing and bring feelings of happiness into your life.

Your emotional intelligence grows when you pay attention to your intuitive knowing which provides valuable information of your inner truth. You recognise that drama and sabotage come from a fear-based need to control, and you learn to let go of this way of living.

Synchronicity abounds when you step onto the unknowable path with only your instincts and intuition to guide you. These synchronicities are a sign that you are on your true path. This guidance is available simply through your ability to hear that small inner voice and acknowledge the feelings that resonate in your heart. The more you learn to trust in these subtle messages the stronger they will grow and the more readily they will arise within you.

Creativity is aligned to magic and this means that it has a habit of unfolding in surprising ways that could not have been predicted.

Creativity is a way of living with aliveness, passion and joy by connecting to the source within that is your authentic self and the freedom of continual new beginnings.

By creating new rituals and ways of being, you heal the heart, feed the soul and allow the authentic essence of your beauty and your truth to express in everyday living.

Sacred Space

Sacred space begins when you create an inner temple where your heart meets your soul. This is a sacred space filled with loving energy where you can come home to your soul's wisdom and a state of peace that is healing to the whole of you. Take time to notice the sacred in the smallest details of your everyday life as you simplify your world and you enter a quiet still place of tranquility inside of you. You will discover how important and valuable it is to give time to this space within and to breath into it. This becomes a state of open receptivity ~ to be still and patient and to wait for inner wisdom to arrive.

CORE ELEMENTS OF A HEROINE'S QUEST

The Heroine's quest is to walk the inner path, to meet herself, to know her truth and hear the wisdom of her soul.

The Heroine's (Hero- in) journey is without a roadmap, the terrain is unknown, details of the outcome cannot be predicted and she must walk this path alone. It is the inner journey into darkness and mystery to meet the feminine within. This is why it requires courage and belief in self. Only then can she learn to tap into the essential feminine that is her creative essence at the core of her being.

When you choose to begin this journey, you will become focused and clear as you learn to trust in the presence of your feminine power.

There comes a time in our lives when questions arise. A period of questioning that comes out of our experience of divine discontent. This searching for answers brings up questions:

What gives shape and meaning to my life?
What makes my heart sing?
What makes my soul glow?
The time arrives for the heroine's to journey begin

A. The heroine's journey often begins with a loss of that which had given your life a shape and meaning and this can become a catalyst for your transformation. What follows is often a period of grief, sadness and disillusionment and you may fall into a place of darkness, a state of depression and experience a loss of all joy in living.

B. Hearing the call. There is an unsettling feeling of being called and an urgency that feels important, which you know in your heart you cannot ignore. (For me, to ignore this calling would have meant that something precious inside of me would die never to be born again.)

C. Starting Over. You step out onto a journey to a destination unknown choosing to leave behind all that is comfortable and familiar. Like the fool in the tarot, you travel light with only your instincts and intuition to guide you.

D. Lessons along the path. The heroine's journey uses an experiential way of teaching important lessons that ultimately bring the seeker to a sense of personal empowerment. It is the path that leads to emotional maturity, where your experiences deepen your relationship to the intelligence hidden within you strengthening your connection to the subtle realms of soul consciousness.

E. The Return Home. This journeying takes time and even though you may lose your way and feel lost, deep down you know that you are becoming an awakened soul. And so you keep owning your truth and speaking from your heart and gradually you learn that your soul is always with you and honours the truth and beauty that is uniquely yours to live. This ultimately brings feelings of empowerment as you integrate somatic wisdom and emotional intelligence and soul guidance. You return home knowing the core essence of your personal soul consciousness.

Self-awareness, self-discovery, seeking a deeper meaning and connecting to the numinous mystery of the unseen world, these are the gifts of taking this heroine's journey.

An awakened soul, shines out of the darkness and emanates a soft golden glow, expressing an innate knowing that bypasses the brain and can be felt deep in your bones and throughout every cell of your body.

Our truth is written in our hearts and is the expression of our soul's presence in today's world. Reclaiming your heart wisdom is coming home to your self as soul. The time has come to step into life as the modern mystic and learn the soul laws of living.

You will know that you have become a Creatress when your heart sings with the happiness of your soul's song and your body dances with joy and wonder as you uncover the intelligence of source within you.

Your soul resonates in your heart
An expression of your beauty and your truth
Your authentic loving self

PART V

*"There are only two ways to live your life
One is as though nothing is a miracle
The other is as though everything is a miracle
I choose the later"*

~ Albert Einstein

8

SOUL LAWS OF LIVING

If soul is the eternal part of each of us then to live guided by messages from soul is to be guided by a wisdom that reaches back into times past and into the future; a wisdom that knows the truth of who you are. Living creatively, loving the pure essence of our truth, holds the power to heal our hearts and heal our soul.

It takes courage to become a seeker of soul suspending old beliefs and risking entering into unknown dimensions. The strength of true empowerment comes from being willing to enter the dark places - to accept that life contains mystery and that there is a power hidden in the darkness that is able to touch into the mystery realms of alchemy and creativity. This energy force is the creative essence that can be found within us all, that holds the secret key to becoming an empowered feminine soul.

A relationship with this inner self begins with listening deeply to the many competing voices that crowd your mind and exist as energy stored in your body influencing how you feel. They are creating the backdrop to the scenes you believe in, they have become your personal story. Notice any negative thoughts and other elements that are creating your current experience.

Being in transition is often painful, bringing feelings of confusion, feeling lost and scared; and without any clear sense of direction; having to let go of everything you thought defined you and gave meaning to your life. This transition phase is the most painful part of the process of re-birth and Individuation, and is the precursor for a shift that brings movement into a new reality; a new becoming and a return to life renewed. It requires you to be real and honest with yourself. Giving yourself permission to feel the depths of your emotions, so that you can move through them, even when it feels like surfing a giant wave. We need to learn to let go and trust in this process. When we become aware that all outer supports seem gone and the only place to go is within, this initiates an invitation that calls us to connect to our own inner strength, power and wisdom.

When you walk alone in the darkness of the underworld, you develop an intimate relationship with yourself and a rich inner life as you tap into a wealth of knowledge that reveals the authenticity of your soul alive in the core of your being.

Transitions happen in darkness. The inner changes are difficult if not impossible to describe to others, if they notice anything at all. You know you are changing and that the strength you are gaining can never be taken away from you.

Connecting to Soul Guidance comes from being kind and loving to the whole of who you are, as a way of becoming real with your Self. Slow down, breathe and connect to the energy of aliveness and stillness within. Instincts, feelings, body speak and other subtle messages await you there.

1. Become grounded in the physical
2. Be present to the world around you
3. Have the courage to feel into your emotions
4. Notice your energy body within and around you
5. Breathe into an inner place to find calmness and peace
6. Notice your inner dialogue – the messages you tell yourself
7. Ask yourself, do I love myself, and do I trust myself?
8. Observe the dreams and images your imagination creates
9. Be open and willing to receiving subtle guidance from your soul

SOUL LANGUAGES

Languages of Soul are sometimes personal and sometimes they arrive as cosmic messages. Listen and learn the languages of your soul as it speaks through you, guiding and loving you. Deep down each of us is a soul who longs to be loved for who we are.

My soul speaks to me in many ways

- Spontaneous words that come out of me unknowingly as I speak

- A song that arrives and repeats in my head and will not leave me
- Flashes of knowing that quickly come and quickly go
- Feelings that well up within me and bring tears to my eyes
- Warmth that enters my heart bringing feelings of joy
- A body that loves to dance and a voice that loves to sing
- A happy child within that loves to dream and play
- Imagination that takes me to new places I have never seen before and dreams that feel real to me
- Signs within my body, like the rush of energy down my spine when I speak a truth to another
- Creativity that arises and feeds the core essence of my feminine self

One of the most powerful things you can learn to do is to *LISTEN* and be receptive to the wisdom of your true inner voice. By Listen, I mean to quieten your mind, become still and open, and attune to energies in and all around you.

The classic movie ET in the 1980's was about an extraterrestrial longing to find his way home. The heart felt phrase "ET phone home" speaks of that longing within each of us to come home to our soul. Being able to tune your dial to listen mode and feel into the energies within you requires that you become relaxed, still, trusting and open. When you take this time to listen to your inner self you open the channel to hearing the voice of your soul. You develop an intimate relationship with yourself as you connect with your inner truth and beauty.

When you give yourself this kind of positive regard, your soul responds by speaking more clearly as it becomes acknowledged, valued and trusted by you.

The greatest gift you can give to another is to truly listen to them so that they feel seen, heard and held by you. This is the path to intimacy with another.

Notice what you believe in and what you honour as important in your life, for this becomes the truth telling of your soul and expresses in the sacredness of your body.

Soul strategies

1. Develop confidence in your own inner knowing as you learn to trust in the messages from your soul.
2. Learn to listen into the whole of yourself as you hear the messages that resonate with your heart.
3. Have the courage to take one small step in the direction your soul is calling.
4. Learn to flow with life as you tune into the natural rhythm of your soul's song.
5. You become the dance as you let go and move to join the flow of the river of life as your trust and confidence grows.

You will notice that synchronicities and magic unfold as you embrace a life guided by the truth in your heart, hearing your soul clearly and feeling your inner soul's glow.

From the day I started to commune with a personal felt sense of my soul my consciousness became forever changed.

> Simplify your life, create space to relax, breathe deeply and open to being guided by soul messages. It is important that you enjoy the journey rather than the destination. I have found that loving yourself means listening to and trusting your self.

We are all part of this dance of life as we learn to flow as one, living in the river of Love

THE POWER OF THE GREAT UNCONSCIOUS

Power is a word that disturbs many of us as we shy away from all the negative connotations that have been placed upon it. I prefer the word empowerment as something that comes from within us rather than being placed upon us by others. Power is a force that exists throughout our world.

There is the power of nature and growing things, the domain of Demeter; the power of delving into the depths of your soul that is Persephone's realm and the power to create your own authentic life story that is the Creatress as she expresses from the pure essence of your inner feminine.

At the beginning of the 20th century a psychologist named Carl Jung began to introduce new terms to describe our inner world and beyond, with words like Anima, Animus, Shadow, Intuition and the Great Unconscious.

He gave us a new understanding that there are feminine and masculine parts within us and each has something different to offer to our quality of living and he introduced the concept of Archetypes as energy constellations alive within us.

Here are some ways of owning our personal power that come from being in touch with the whole of our self. This effects how we relate to ourselves with positive self-talk and loving self-regard and gives us the power to reshape our world.

The Power of Inner dialogue:

Take time to listen to your inner dialogue, the words you are speaking to yourself. We teach others how to treat us by the way we treat ourselves. So it follows that to shape new behaviours we need to shape new dialogues in our inner world as the first step to any real change. We set our intentions by the way in which we talk to ourselves. True power to change our lives lies within each of us. Each tiny step, freely chosen, to walk in a new direction, has the power to create a new reality and a new sense of self.

The Power of Inner Focus

When we focus our attention, we shine an inner light to illuminate our truth. This opens us to an inner source of knowledge and information, to guide us to know who we are becoming on our soul journey.

Self-reflection is a mix of meditation and action as a practical way of connecting our inner and outer worlds. Taking time for self-reflection is a valuable way to create a relationship to your inner wisdom. Reflective writing is a way to access inner wisdom by holding a question lightly and clearing a space so you can observe what arises from within. By posing a question and listening inwardly, an inner voice or emotion arises as you meditate upon this question. As thoughts and feelings arise into your consciousness, take up your pen and write them down. Then go back into an inner focused state and continue to stay relaxed, receptive and listening, and repeat the process until you feel complete.

The Power of Emotions

Heart energy is intelligent creative energy and emotions are (e-motion) as energy in motion there to be felt and to be used as fuel for our creativity. Imagination provides creative inspiration. So colour the image you hold with an emotional charge and move courageously in the direction of your dreams.

The Power of Imagination infuses every part of us and feeds – our emotions, our energy body and our mind. It is the food of fertility and creativity and it expresses itself easily through the mediums of art. Learn how to use imagination wisely and be aware of its power to influence thoughts, feelings and outcomes in our lives.

The Power of Story

As we begin to tell our story we discover our personal truth. Stories personalise our lives and teach us how to live. They can bring alive a sense of the heroine who inspires us to be brave and become more than we thought possible.

Bodies are primal containers that register our knowingness and store memories of lessons learned, that become the stories we repeatedly tell ourselves. Stories, parables, metaphors, dreams and spiritual truths can feed the Imagination. They hold the power to bring clarity and nourishment to enrich your soul.

The Power of Trans-Personal Cosmic Forces

By awakening all your senses, you connect to your soul. This allows the universal intelligence of Source to speak to you. Be willing to let this energy flow through you and follow its guidance for this is how you partner with the Great Unconscious.

The Power of Sleep

As we sleep we shift into an altered state of consciousness where we become able to partner with the Great Unconscious. The power of sleep can bring us gifts of healing, learning and growing. Take time to rest and recuperate and give time for the great unconscious to do its work while you sleep. Hand over problems to sleep - insights and creative connections often arise on awakening and you find that problems have often been solved gracefully while you slept. The trick is to be ready to catch these new insights upon waking. Sleep opens up a place for Dreams and Intuition to come more easily to us especially when we are rested, relaxed and open. Dream work is the processing and grounding of dream images, often by using active Imagination. Psychology can help to give context and to ground new perspectives and to integrate them to becoming part of your life. In Jungian dream work, every part of the dream can be taken to mirror something of your inner self and it is often the emotional charge attached to dream imagery that tells an important story.

The Power of Space

It is the space, the emptiness between that feeds the creative process. It is an emptiness that is not empty, a space to reach beyond our conscious mind into a state that is rich with potentiality of inspiration from the unknowable beyond that is the universal intelligence of source.

Space and Time to Be

Making space for silence, sitting in solitude is a state of aloneness that is not loneliness.

The music of love and the cosmos speaks to us within this silence, which is not silent. Hear the song of your soul and feel into all that awakens you to awareness of your subtle energy body vibrating with your truth.

Being in solitude can provide a quality of presence that is the experience of Kairos time. Being in the present, in a state of heightened consciousness - a time between, where we lose our sense of chronological time. (clock-time as we know it.)

The experience of space can be on the physical, mental, emotional or imagined level of awareness. With this openness to space on all levels, you can shift your focus onto:

- Making friends with your soul
- Showing kindness to your self
- Trusting in the unfolding flow of your soul life
- Becoming sensitive to energy in and around you
- Listening and feeling into your feminine power

Find your own temple/sanctuary, a place where you can commune with your inner self to hear the voices of your soul.

Some find peace in the forest
Some love their connection to the ocean
Some love to sit beside a still deep lake
Others like to search the stars and connect to the vastness of the cosmos

And some like a cozy corner in a quiet room

Choose your favourite space and go there often

The Power of Naming
The power of naming new archetypes creates an identity we become aware of as an energy force that we can personally begin to relate to in our everyday lives. This holds the power to uplift and inspire us just as art and symbols can awaken us to new levels of awareness of the beauty within us.

The Power of Images and Symbols
Feminine Images and Symbols can feed the embodiment of empowered feminine presence. Venus is famous for the girdle she wore around her waist as a symbol of her feminine beauty and power. Symbols can reflect new insights gained and carry many layers of meaning. So find something that speaks to your heart as a symbol of you as an empowered Creatress. It could be a hat, a belt, a ring, or other piece of jewellery, or some clothing in your best colour that symbolises this empowered feminine energy for you. When you put it on every time you step out into the world, this then becomes your secret code to yourself and to the Universe of who you truly are.

Finding images that represent new energy coming into your life is a wonderful way of reminding yourself who you are as a soul. I have an image of a breakthrough angel on my wall that I bought years ago at the Angel Sanctuary in Alet les Bains in France. Create a treasure board to capture an overview of the symbols that speak to your heart.

There is a power in symbols that connect us to our imagination without the need for words and there is simplicity of truth to the many layers of meaning they contain. Where art and imagination combine, as in symbolic images seen in the Tarot – such as Rider Waite Tarot, Earth Magic cards, Inner child cards and many more. Tarot can be a tool to awaken us to intuitive and psychic messages.

Cosmic Power and Astrology

I have grown to understand the world through the lens of astrology and I know astrology as a profound language of energy and a symbolic language of our psyche.

Astrology speaks the truth of our soul's potential with symbols that are rich with multiple layers of meaning. These astrological symbols reveal themselves to us when we are ready to receive their archetypal wisdom.

The energy map of your birth is a blueprint of your soul's essence symbolically describing the potentiality of your life's story. Its patterns of energy are alive within each of us and are shown visually by this ancient symbolic language expressed in the birth chart.

Soul speaks to us through all dimensions of our being, and chooses the elements that resonate most closely with our unique planetary elemental mix. We experience our self through the four elements of earth, air, water and fire as soul consciousness that resonates within every part of our psyche.

Functions and Symbols of the Four Elements

Air ~ Mind and the intellectual world of words and constructs. Air guides with messages through the airways as words like *a bird in flight*
Water ~ Emotions and the world of ever changing

moods and memories. Water nurtures emotions that *flow like a river.*
Earth ~ Body/soma and the physical world of form and the Earth protects as *Mother Gaia and nature.*
Fire ~ Imagination and the world of passions, colours and images that inspire. Fire inspires and energizes with Imagination as art with *movement and dance.*

The Fire Element is the rogue element that can appear to be wildly passionate and sometimes uncontrollable. Fire is our imagination that has the power to feed our fears as well as our passions. Thoughts that come from imagination are not only very real but also manifestly powerful, so we need to use them wisely and with care, and only for our highest good.

A 5th elemental dimension is our subtle body, that manifest into our psychic energy field. This brings together the whole self as our energy blueprint that surrounds us. Our soul's truth resonates throughout our Etheric body and shows in our Aura (our personal energy field), mirroring our souls's highest potential. Questions to ask your self :

1. What is the image I hold of myself? – Imagination/Fire.
2. What words do I speak to myself? – Mind /Air.
3. What emotions do I feel within me? – Emotions/Water
4. How do I embody myself and claim my space? – Body/Earth
5. What is my energy field messaging to others? – Psyche/Aura. Your energy gestalt ~ the whole of you

The answers to these questions will speak the story of your

true essence. Gaining a sense of yourself as soul comes from tuning in moment by moment to the whole of you and deep learning comes from experiential whole body knowing.

The psychic mediums that relate to each of these elemental forces are:

> Fire ~Clairvoyance ~ clear seeing
> Air ~ Clairaudience ~ clear hearing
> Water ~ Clair-Sentience ~ clear sensing
> Earth ~ Clair-Cognisance ~ clear knowing

The element that is most dominant for me is air and so I find that clairaudience is my predominant soul language, as intuition brings messages that arrive spontaneously into my consciousness. My only past regret is not listening to them more often. The more I accept this part of me as valid and true, the stronger this guidance has grown within me.

Energy is E-motion that is empowering as it informs us of our inner essence.

Our bodies are mostly made of empty space and then there is water which is the medium for rapidly transmitting energy vibrations through space and time. We are energy with a frequency and a vibration that is uniquely our own. The quality of the relationship we have with our emotional body affects the quality of our vibrational energy field, expressed in our subtle energy body and seen as our auric field.

The core essence of feminine creativity manifests energy into the physical dimension that has a slower vibrational energy we recognise as physical forms we can see, know, touch, taste and feel with our senses.

We become grounded when we connect to the earth. This allows us to more easily become present and real as physical beings. Just as electricity races into the earth, so too any overload of energy in our bodies dissipates when we stand barefooted on the earth. By connecting to nature in this way we are able to release any negative energy we have absorbed that can leave us feeling distracted, depleted and unfocused. Just like plants we need to be grounded, with our roots connected to the soil of the earth, to be able to grow strong and true.

Inner Thoughts are actively present much of the time. Their energy as thought forms are as real for us as physical forms are real. Ask yourself if your thoughts are love based and if they are, listen deeply and take in the clarity of their message for they are a powerful force.

Emotions speak the language of our heart. If they are fear based then we need to listen deeper, to uncover the story they are attached to. Going deeper into our emotions can reveal the need that is hidden beneath the fear, so it can be acknowledged and any pain attached to it felt so that its negative hold over us can be released.

Our sensitivity grows as we become more conscious of our feelings, our body, our emotions and the intuitive and psychic knowings of our inner world.

As this sensitivity to energies grows, we become more finely attuned to subtle changes in energies in and around us and we find ourselves sensing the emotions of those close to us.

It becomes important to be conscious of what is ours and what belongs to another. This creates the need to have clear psychic boundaries, to protect ourselves and to limit our attunement to undesirable energies so that we are able to choose what we let in and what we protect ourselves from.

It can take some practice to separate out what is our own truth and to release the feelings we have taken on from others. We are capable of empathy for self and others when we have clear boundaries and feel grounded and safe to express ourselves and protect ourselves.

Instead of being busy doing, take time to be busy being. It is important to take time to rest, recuperate and integrate our experiences. Down time, extra sleep, time to dream and process, time to ask for guidance and handing over our cares to let the unconscious do its work for you. Taking time to sleep on important decisions is giving the great unconscious realms of intelligence a chance to assist you to find just the right answer for you.

This Inner Journey to meet yourself as a body of energy vibrating at your own frequency also magnifies your sensitivity to other vibrational fields of energy. Your body is the sacred temple of your soul, so treat it well, listen to it, feed it, care for it and keep it safe. Only when we take time to listen to our inner voice, value it, trust in it, and allow ourselves to be guided by it, can we claim the true power of the feminine within us, with her Soul Messages.

Personal Soul is our connection to the Cosmic Intelligence of Source

PART VI

Your heart begins to dance and sing with joy
As it resonates with the wisdom of your soul
Awaken to the unique sparkle of your Truth
Follow your Heart; hear the voices of your Soul
And Love the Feminine within you

10

SOUL LIFE OF A MODERN MYSTIC

Embracing the dance of life as magical mystery

A Modern Mystic knows how to live between two worlds, the outer world of form and actions and the inner world of invisible mystery that holds the key that opens the door to a life of soul consciousness. The relationship you have with yourself is mirrored by the quality of the relationships you experience with those around you. When you desire to create a new reality then the place to start is inside of yourself.

By choosing the path of becoming an awakened soul, you have learned to live by a different set of guidelines and you have walked the path of the heroine's quest. You then discover that your soul knows you intimately and wants you to live your truth, experience fulfilment and find your joy.

Life becomes much simpler in some ways, as you tune into the values you hold true to your heart. The more difficult challenge comes in learning to trust in your own inner knowing and to step outside of society's plans and onto the path of the fool, guided by your open heart and a beginner's instinctual wisdom.

It takes courage and commitment to keep faith with yourself when you cannot explain where you are going or why to others. You don't know the outcome but you feel intensely called to take the journey into the unknown realms of mystery.

As synchronicities unfold before you and your connection to the voices of your soul grows, you become stronger in your convictions that you are on the right path. You are learning that real change is an inside job and you take quiet time often, to reflect on the new ways in which you are creating meaning to your life.

You know your inner world is where all true change begins. As you create a natural routine where you nurture and care for yourself, you commit to your own way of living that is uniquely yours. You are learning to love your soul in all its shades of lightness and darkness. When you give yourself permission to love the whole of who you are, you become a Creatress and you mirror the beauty of your soul in how you live in every moment and this reawakens your joyful, creative inner child self.

THE WAYS OF A MODERN MYSTIC

A modern mystic develops her subtle senses so that she can feel her way in the darkness. She connects with her body, its instincts and wisdom; her emotions and her imagination; and she strengthens her trust in her intuitive and psychic knowing.

The inner relationship she has with herself is one of positive self-regard. She knows how to be kind and loving to herself and she lives guided by the intelligence of her heart. She listens deeply and can see beneath the surface of words that are spoken. She notices her inner dialogue as it affirms what is real and true for her. She knows her inner world well and this sets the ground for her to create her unique soul story.

She is comfortable with paradox and mystery and she knows how to hold space open for something new to emerge. Imagination is her friend as the impulse/passion that feeds and stimulates her creation processes.

She loves the Earth as the ground of her being that supports her and she follows her heart as it guides her with the truth of her soul. Heart and Earth are made up of the same letters and they both contain the word ART within them. The three are all connected as parts of the same whole that is the creative expression of our personal soul, as it manifests by bringing new forms to life. Art to her is an expression from her soul.

She is willing to let go and release her old self and risk entering into the darkness of the unknowable mystery of the Other/Underworld. She finds herself experiencing joy as she lives her creative and authentic life and she becomes the very best version of herself that she can be.

She may be a priestess; teacher of the sacred way, made possible by her intense high vibrational attunement and her presence lifts the energy vibrations of those around her.

The energy of love is the highest vibrational field we can experience as humankind here on earth

Raising ourselves to a higher vibrational energy and living a life of passionate involvement, gives us the power to impact the vibrational energy of humanity with the truth and beauty of our presence.

As you set new intentions you change your vibrational field and the old illusionary state of mind is lost and you become able to create new images encompassing your vision for a new way of living and a life connected to source and soul.

Be open to honouring your sensitivity and your gifts that have been hidden within you. Then you will find yourself accomplishing tasks with ease and grace.

Our ancestors connect to us through our soul. They are the keepers of the earth watching over us from the other world of Cosmic Soul.

Looking back you see that you knew when you were ready to follow the calling of your soul as feelings of divine discontent arose in you.

As you find the courage to follow these subtle promptings, not only must you be willing to go into the darkness of unknowable mystery but also to open yourself to being guided by forces you cannot fully perceive.

As your trust in this other intelligence grows and you take small steps in a new direction, you will find there are synchronicities to light your way and ease your path.

EXPERIENCES OF BECOMING A MODERN MYSTIC

A modern mystic is she who is comfortable with the Mysteries, lives guided by her inner wisdom and is open to guidance from the Intelligence of the Cosmos.

She gives herself the luxury of sitting in silence, to listen within and she lives guided by her inner wisdom. She is connected to her personal truth and the energy of Source that knows the becoming of her soul.

Her whole body informs her of its inner wisdom that is source intelligence within her. She is willing to enter the domain of dark mystery where she touches into the unknowable world of the unfathomable 'Other.'

Another name for a modern mystic is a Persephone woman ~ she who is at home with ancient mysteries and the rebirthing of feminine empowerment in today's world.

She owns her feminine power and is visibly creating her unique soul story, in ways that honour the sacredness of everyday living, and her innocence and wisdom combine in a creative dance of becoming.

THE OUTCOME OF LIVING AS A MODERN MYSTIC

It is time for us to overcome unconsciously held beliefs from our past and acknowledge their power to keep us stuck in an endless repeating reality.

> *When we give ourselves permission to live creatively and boldly walk into the future and even to fail sometimes, we are validating the calling of our soul*

A Modern Mystic learns the soul lessons hidden beneath the veil of her outer self. They empower her feminine presence as she honours the invisible and subtle realms of feminine consciousness. She knows how to:

- Step back, detach, depersonalise and breath into calmness
- Go within for answers and connect to the wisdom of her soul
- Awaken to a wider perspective and an expanded picture of reality
- Trust in guidance when it comes in subtle ways
- Feel the love within her, it is her inner soul's glow

She becomes a mentor to others; and by her presence she empowers them to embrace a life of soul consciousness.

Her way of being is to embrace the dance of life and live creatively, in its flow with aliveness, spontaneity and simplicity. Synchronicities she experiences may seem like magic. This is how she creates a new soul story for herself.

Embrace a life of creativity and originality

A NEW WORLD VIEW

Becoming

We are a mystery unfolding in
The dimensions of space and time
With the task to become a unique soul
As expression of Source here on Earth
To listen to our Heart and to know at last
How to embrace Becoming as the Magic of Art

We are here to become en-souled beings, with our physical body in service to our soul. You have a golden glow at the core of your being and like the sparkle of a new star, you are here to shine the light of your truth and let your beauty show. The world becomes at peace when we all come together as unique soul stars in friendship and love.

Living as a Creatress requires a new worldview, as you own your voice, claim your space and step into your feminine power. Ask yourself this question:

What lights me up and energises me so my inner light glows?

Tune in and listen to your soul's wisdom and notice that which makes your heart sing. And then take the risk to follow the truth in your heart, one small step at a time, living in the flow, as it unfolds before you.

As you travel this path of soul consciousness you will find that your life flows in surprising directions, leading you effortlessly towards your fulfilment and joy.

You will experience a clarity and simplicity to your life, as your energy increases and your heart begins to heal.

You become the source of your own light as it intensifies within you, making your eyes shine and your aura glow.

When traveling alone you step outside of your comfort zone and you meet with your inner truth that carries the power and simplicity to set you free.

The innate gift of being an outcast, when you have nothing left to lose is to be able to live your truth, free to become the unique and wonderful you that you have come to this earth to become, your soul star self.

When we are alone and give ourselves quiet inner focused, reflective time, we are learning to hear and to trust in the subtle messages that come from within. We receive these subtle messages through intuition that flashes into our consciousness and other forms of guidance that resonate as a knowing in our body as deep feelings of our truth.

Essence and Meaning

It is not until some time has past that the meaning of your long journey comes together and you find you have found your voice and your connection to universal wisdom. You now have the ability to live a life of soul consciousness, claiming the gift of freedom to live an authentic life filled with creativity, happiness and joy that arise from within.

> Your soul shines with the light of your truth and the forever-pure essence of you, as a golden glow with the power to reach into the hearts of others.

As you embrace the alchemy of becoming a Creatress you will find that others will be attracted to you who mirror the person you have become.

Myths of Empowerment
Both Psyche and Persephone entered the dark, hidden realms of the underworld and returned again to their lives in the upper world.
By entering this transformational zone they have faced the pain of their losses and they have become changed by their experiences. This inner journey has empowered them to become creative feminine women who know how to own their truth and the beauty of their soul.

To be a goddess is to become immortal. It is our soul that is the immortal part of us that can never be truly lost or destroyed, it merely changes form as it passes between the physical realm of time and space and the indescribable dimension of cosmic soul to rejoin the primordial energy of Source. It is through the dark feminine that we enter the transition zone between these realms and find answers that carry the potential to heal our soul.

*The Black Virgin Statues I found in France
awakened me to the dark feminine and her
qualities of Virgin ~ meaning she belongs to
herself alone, she is her own mistress with the
power to choose for herself*

*She does not feel inferior to the masculine, she
is empowered from within herself,
in command of her own voice, she stands in
her own power as equal and other to the
masculine*

*Her wisdom comes from her experiences of the
dark mysteries of life, the natural cycles of
death and rebirth and her intimate
relationship with her soul*

*Black Virgin statues of mother and child
symbolise the loving healing power of the
feminine as mother, matter, earth and
creativity expressed in her child*

*The Black Virgin represents the pure
essence of feminine empowerment
Like a well-spring of purest water that
arises from a place deep within the earth.*

*I believe that creativity is her core,
the fountain of her pure essence,
her power to manifest new forms
and her connection to source.*

~

THE AGE OF THE MODERN MYSTIC HAS ARRIVED.

A Modern Mystic enters a world beyond the veil of mystery and opens the way to magic by living as a Creatress in tune with the rhythm of her soul. She knows how to dance in the river of love and she embraces the sacredness of life and the unfolding cycles of creativity as they express through her physical presence.

As a Creatress, she has matured into her feminine self by developing her emotional intelligence, so she can choose her actions wisely rather than re-act to the world around her. She knows the importance of developing a relationship with her inner self and to reflect upon her experiences in a way that is honest, real and true, to gain new perspectives and to find the courage to empathise with the feelings of others.

A modern mystic is her own mistress, she is virgin in the sense of being one-in-herself and she has learned how to shape shift between two worlds, that of the sacred and the mundane.

The archetype of the Creatress leads to an expansion of consciousness of the creative power of the feminine within us all. The Creatress speaks directly to us sharing her wisdom and her loving presence. We are in essence both personal and universal and our wise soul knows that source is within each of us.

As we enter this place of emotional depth and intimacy to our inner self we connect with innate Intelligence that is within and all around us. By loving and valuing the feminine we restore our connection to the immortal essential core of the Feminine.

We each are a glowing light, a soul star of the night sky,

unique in our aliveness as the pure feminine essence of our sacred soul.

> *"Go deeper within and ask yourself ~ "Who am I?"*
> *Your soul knows the answer to your question*
> *A Sacred ~ Heart Centered ~ Soul*

PART VII

*"To this joyous festival of creation,
Thou must contribute thy most precious treasure
In that work of creation, thou willst discover
Thy own store of riches that lie hidden in thee."*

*~ Rabindranath Tagore
Poems from Mohuā
The Herald of Spring*

12

HAPPINESS AND CONNECTION TO SOURCE

The core essence of the feminine is creativity and her search for meaning becomes a search for the aliveness of a loving heart.

Happiness is a whole body experience that lightens and uplifts your soul with an inner feeling that makes your heart want to sing. Happiness may be many things to many people as it passes through us, awakening an inner sense of peace and joy.

Subtle messages can so easily be misunderstood or ignored completely and yet when we stop and listen, in time they really do make sense. An intuition carries a rightness to it that resonates with the truth that feels deeply real that we carry in our hearts.

We take pills to mask our symptoms and to blot out our pain, living in a world of avoidance and denial. Our pain – physical, emotional, mental, imaginal or psychic – carries important messages from our soul. It is only by delving into our pain that we begin to uncover our truth. It is this truth that can set us free as self-awareness leads to self-responsibility and the gifts of maturity, authenticity and empowerment.

Your soul knows the truth of who you are here to become and will guide your journey, if you have the courage to listen and follow her subtle messages. She knows how to lead you on what may seem to be a meandering pathway, so that you gather the experiences you need to create a foundation for you to create your unique soul story.

The pathway through is to sit with the discomfort of not knowing, holding a clear intention for good, with the willingness to receive guidance and to patiently wait until inspiration and intuition arises. This may come as an inner knowing that feels right and true, as an emotion that surfaces to reveal the true depth of your feelings or your body may speak to you with its innate wisdom.

Permission given to yourself, to become the holder of your vision for your highest self, creates the possibility to release negative energy blocks from stored memories that hold power to create tension, resistance and pain in your body.

When another can see the potential hidden within you, and believes in your dream for you, they then hold you accountable for your actions as they energise that vision of your potentiality. This can become a great motivator for you to expand into becoming the best you that you can be.

If this mentor is missing in your life then the task is for you to become that cheerleading fan for yourself.

FEMININE CREATIVITY & SOUL

All creativity begins in the unseen realms of darkness. Universal truths of our time exist all around us, waiting to be plucked from the ether and brought into consciousness.

The darkness of our inner world contains riches and is the fertile ground for creativity, where we uncover our soul's inner glow. As we dance in the river of life experiencing flowing synchronicities can seem like magic. Magic is an essential element of creativity.

I have always loved the ocean, and especially when there are waves. The waves of the ocean are like the waves of the cosmos – cosmic waves of love that have the power to wash through us, changing us, making us awaken to our passion for life itself. When we take that passion and live creatively in each moment, the intelligence of the cosmos awakens in us and is there to guide our way. When we are willing to move forward, letting go that which no longer serves us, we then create space for the new to reveal itself as we move one step closer to our dream. What stops us is how we judge ourselves and deny ourselves permission to dance with life.

I see life as a dance of energy that is constantly flowing and I like to think of our lives as being like a river that is forever unfolding as it finds its way. I am learning that it is the journey itself that becomes the river of my life. So remember to enjoy the journey with all its twists and turns, its blocks and stagnant hollows and its ever-flowing current that draws us all along.

OUR COSMOS/UNIVERSE

There is more to our cosmos than we can ever imagine or know. Source is an originating dimension beyond consciousness we cannot understand with our limited perceptions; an unknowable force, an intelligence and an energy system beyond time and space, primordial essence in potentiality of the mysteries of all creation.

It is beyond dualities such as masculine and feminine, day and night, sun and moon, and the dimensions of time and space. Source is the universe that lives within us all and Source is the home of Cosmic soul when our soul no longer has a physical form.

Bring balance and harmony to our world

When we live a life that mirrors the truth within our soul, we become aware that we are living creatively in every moment.

"I feel a well of happiness arise within me, and feelings of joy wash over me. I experience happiness, which I cannot not easily explain that bubbles up inside me and I find myself spontaneously bursting into song without realising it. I feel a harmony with everything in the world around me. I am energy vibrating in space."

> **Warning:** The philosophy expressed in this book is not guaranteed to create a life of conformity and may not always fulfil the many traditional expectations of society. It can however bring a sense of purpose and overwhelming joy into your life.

It takes courage to walk the path of the Creatress, willing to trust in your inner wisdom and following the guidance of your soul. It is a quest into your inner world in search for meaning that lies at the heart of all Matter and is your path to uncover your personal Creative Feminine Essence.

Cosmic Intelligence comes to us as simple truth that seems obvious once we learn to perceive it.

BEFRIEND FEMININE POWER AND DON THE MANTLE OF A CREATRESS

Becoming a Creatress is not something you put on like a hat or a new gown. It is something that you become, something deeply connected to the soul within you, not something found outside of you. It is your connection to a relationship with your inner wise self as soul and becomes your link to guidance from cosmic intelligence from the great beyond.

Cosmic guidance resonates as source within you, so value your inner wisdom and know that source intelligence is also within you.

You don't need to ask others, as you already know the answers. Your soul's energy is in and all around you; it speaks through you and is able to guide you when you have learned how to trust in its amazing wisdom.

Don't forget to ask for guidance and give yourself time to develop trust in your ability to listen and to hear this wisdom and know this is the intelligence of your soul. You will find that change can come quickly and gracefully, it does not have to be painful or from extended periods of hard effort.

The ultimate aim is to create a habit of being able to shift your focus in any moment in time, by fluidly moving between inner and outer perceptions so this becomes a part of your everyday way of living, The more your relationship with your inner self grows the stronger is your connection to Source within and beyond. This becomes a way of life incorporating the qualities of Simplicity and Truth as you hone down into your essence to find your hidden beauty with a listening ear for the voice of your soul.

Dance is as ancient as humankind. It is a primary and fundamental expression of who we are and has been part of ancient primitive cultures from the beginning of time. It may even pre-date language as a way of communicating and bringing people together. There is music in the universe and in the unfolding energy of my soul, which can be expressed spontaneously through dance with graceful movements.

Watching birds perform their mating rituals, they amaze and delight us with their dance. Movement connects us to our physicality, the energy within us, and awakens us to our emotions; creating energy, expressing passion and feeling fully alive in the moment. As we communicate through dance, it helps us to be fluid, flexible, agile and nimble in the ways we respond to this ever-changing world.

"We don't have to do it all alone.
Being present in the moment with trust in our inner knowing and
our connection to source
Practical & magical mysteries combine and we become more
than we ever imagined our selves to be."

Each person's path is intimately unique to them, and it follows archetypal patterns that involve a meeting with the alchemy of creativity in darkness. The time is now, to create a new relationship with darkness as the essence of all that is feminine and to grow into becoming your soul. Living a life of Soul involves making friends with our darkness, for darkness contains the magic of creativity and the gold of hidden treasure within you is the pure glow of your soul.

Emotional Intelligence comes from knowing the languages of your heart and an awareness of messages from your body. They are the realms of Feminine intelligence.

Gather the power of your beauty and truth, become a Creatress and know that your soul is the pure and loving essence of your immortal truth that extends throughout all space and time.

When there is a deep and loving experience of positive self regard, you find yourself willing to risk becoming a Creatress, by giving the universe permission to guide you on your own unique soul story. Then and only then have you found your yellow brick road, the pathway to happiness and the way home to your soul self.

This book could not have been written had I not first written *Odyssey of a Creatress*, for this story came out of the writing of the other; this is the nature of the creative process in action. I now feel able to create my world in alignment with my soul and find new meaning to my life's journey. The path I took was long, to reclaim the sacred mystery of my Feminine Soul. I now know the Feminine as the essential nature of all that is invisible, creative, magical and alive at the heart of all Matter.

> '*By connecting to the mystery of your soul,*
> *You will be able to make empowering choices,*
> *Create new meaning, and experience peace and*
> *Happiness arising spontaneously within you*'

CREATIVITY, IMAGINATION AND ART

What is creativity and what role does imagination and art play in life as a Creatress so that she is able to live creatively and in connection to

EARTH ~ HEART ~ ART

All Creativity begins in the unseen realms of darkness and evolves out of the experience of flowing with the What Is of life. Being fully present, going with the natural flow of energy, you learn to trust in your own inner wisdom and let it guide you on your journey to becoming a joyful and loving creative soul.

There is a moment when the creative process takes over with its own momentum. This is when magic happens and the unexpected occurs, arising from the energy field of creativity, and spontaneity becomes a natural way of living.

Imagination precedes intention and is the initiating stimulus

for creativity that is fed by the power of an image, a vision, an idea or a dream.

How do you use your imagination ~ to feed your fears or to feed your dreams?

Art has the power to move us and bring up all kinds of feelings and sensations that resonate with our hearts and help us to work out who we are and what holds meaning for us. We can each have a different experience from seeing the same art. Soul communicates through dreams and visions using symbols and images. They stimulate our imagination with ideas and insights, all of which come to us from Source.

When we are young, our imaginations are wild and free and we believe that anything is possible as we become curious and feel into the joy of the inner playful child and believe that magic is a natural part of life itself.

Our body and especially our heart, gives us a place to connect with the intelligence of source. We can retrain ourselves to hear our heart's voice as this intelligence. The gift of our pure essence is the energy of source that lives within us waiting to be revealed. It is up to us to have the courage to own it. As we mature into our soul awareness, our heart becomes joyful, light and free.

Michelangelo says about sculpting the statue of David that it was his task to uncover the form of David in the stone waiting to be revealed, so that its beauty could be seen by others. This is also so of our soul life buried within us.

Julia Cameron's *The Artists Way* and *The Vein of Gold* are both wonderful books with exercises that can open the door to unleashing the artist within each of us.

There is an ancient art of mending a broken vase in Japan called *Kintsugi*, which translated means 'golden joinery.' The broken pieces are put back together so that the vase becomes restored with threads of gold. The finished vase is then more beautiful than before it was broken.

Mystery is an essential element of Creativity. I think of Black as the colour that contains all colours, now I make friends with the unknowable mystery of my darkness knowing it holds many gifts from my soul.

Pierre Soulage (Soul Age) was a French artist who created from the core of his being, allowing each work to emerge from some place deep within him.

Pierre thought of his art as including the canvas, himself and the energy field it induces through the rapport of black with the light. Although he painted with only the colour black, his paintings are of subtle shades of light and darkness and he calls himself the painter of light.

His philosophy was "I wait till I dare." Allowing the magical moment beyond intention to reveal the unexpected is an expression of the pure essence of the creative process itself. It is the acceptance of failure and imperfection that opens up the journey to allow something surprising to arise. This is the nature of miracles and of creativity in action.

After many years of exploration he came across a very personalised style of painting that he called Outrenoir (Meaning –

French for 'beyond black',) which he describes as painting light as energy that comes out of blackness.

He is known as the painter of the light and his black works express something of the mystery that is the primal essence of life itself; cosmic darkness, the velvet black that is present before light, in the dark void of cosmic consciousness. Without blackness the light cannot speak and in Soulage's Outrenoir the light speaks to us out of the darkness. Our experience of his work changes as we move and shift our perspective to it.

There are stories of men painting in the total blackness of caves and they painted with black. The images that emerged out of the darkness remind us of ancient art as primal instinct and pure creative expression motivated by a desire to know who we are and where we come from and record our world for others to see.

Art is subjective and each person sees something different in the same piece. Its beauty is in the way it speaks to our soul and awakens our hearts to the awareness of the immense power of authenticity, stories of mankind's experiences, expressing love as images.

Black is maternal. It is in darkness that new life is conceived, incubated and formed. It is a blackness that is rich with potentiality of all that is or will ever be. I refer to this mirrored dimension of darkness as universal Source. Creative processes need darkness for something new to come into being. Therefore we need to let go of the overriding negativity towards darkness and move beyond fear into a trust in something far greater than our small ego-driven selves can ever know.

We need this new relationship to blackness, quiet inner-focused time, a return of innocence and wonder, a willingness to risk, to have the courage and to listen to our soul and follow its callings. A heart-centred life comes from developing trust in the mystery and wisdom that resides in our feminine soul.

Each of us is a unique expression of the cosmic whole and we each carry a gift hidden in the depths of our soul. Are you courageous enough to take the journey inwards to become one with the core essence of who you are as the unique you? The best you that you can become is waiting to be unveiled and only you can walk the path of awareness to the truth and beauty of your soul. This is the path to a deep connection to the energy of source that is alive within you and carries an intelligence one could liken only to genius.

All of life becomes a meditation when we live in the dance of life, allowing energy to flow like water finding its path across the land. We have been conned into believing that all wisdom and power exists outside of the self. In fairy tales where the princess is awakened by the kiss of the prince/rescuer, this is where her story ends. We do not get to see her claim her inner power and mature into becoming a Queen. This requires choosing the Inner journey and learning to love and trust your self.

THE OUTCOME OF LIVING A LIFE OF SOUL

Personal Truth and honesty mean being real with yourself and allowing your true feelings to surface, so that they can be acknowledged and felt. If they feel too overwhelming to process alone then the sharing of your truth with a trusted other can be of enormous help in processing the buried emotions that have been clouding your perceptions of reality.

Being willing to let go of old stories and memories of the past becomes possible as you begin to learn how powerful your intentions can be. How you use your imagination is of crucial importance. Your imagination is so powerful and carries the ability to create your reality. Every thought and every feeling is run through your awareness as you ask yourself ~

"Is this the reality I wish to create for myself?"

The Black Feminine carries the energies of the great mother. Her power is that of Magnetic energy, the great attractor within the earth. She can be likened to the negative charge at the South Pole of the earth, this place found opposite to the North Pole, which carries a positive charge. She is negative in the sense of mystery and hidden power. Acceptance of her darkness and her inner glow are expressions of being an awakened soul.

Pierre Soulage, the master of Outrenoir – of Black and Light, uses no colour to manipulate light. When light is reflected on black, it transforms and transmutes it. His art captures the dark essence and mystery of the feminine principle and expresses her power visually.

Barbara Brennan describes the energy of Black Velvet as a special healing quality of blackness she uses in energy healing, in her book *Hands Of Light*.

∾

The Cosmos is within as the source of your unique soul star

self and your truth has the power to heal you, bringing the intelligence of your feelings and mind into relationship, as you re-member your true self and by doing so you become whole. This is whole body energy healing that heals your heart and also heals your soul.

Empowerment comes from choosing to own your truth and finding your voice in whatever way that may be, activating the creative essence within you is an act of faith and trust in yourself and in the cosmos as your guiding partner in creativity.

Life becomes the art and each person's path is intimately unique to them alone, although it follows archetypal patterns and involves the alchemy of creativity in the darkness.

PROFILE OF THE PURE ESSENTIAL FEMININE

You will know that you have become a Creatress when your heart sings with the happiness of your soul's song and your body dances with joy and wonder as you discover that you have source within you and your soul's light glows.

As you develop your own personal mythology and walk the mystical path you will begin to see that you are not alone. There are many others taking this journey to connect to their pure essential self and to shine the light of their soul.

Feminine Essence
She is innocent and wise; fierce and loving; courageous and kind; playful and passionate; honouring her personal truth and guided by her soul.
She has a light within that sparkles with playfulness, she is relaxed as she dances with a graceful flow

Your soul lets you know when you are on your true soul path. It lights up a glow within you and shines through your laughing eyes in a way that cannot be manufactured by taking a drug. It lifts your heart and you become so light that you start to feel you could fly as if on angels' wings.

My hope is that you now know how important time spent getting to know your inner 'Me' really is. Only the pure energy of love has the power to light up your inner soul's glow.

Love yourself, love what you do, loving who you are becoming. True love begins with your self and is the great connector and the greatest power on earth. Fear cannot exist when your soul is glowing with love.

Your soul can guide you in ways that carry you into Kairos time, a state beyond time and space where your ego sense of self is lost as you enter a place of creativity. From this place it is possible to experience numinous moments of connection to the Source energy of the cosmos. Relax into being present to energy in every moment, descend into Kairos time and connect to the energy of source. Be one with nature, breathe into the energy of what is; flow with the unfolding dance of life, in tune with the music of the cosmos. This is how you can reach a state of Gnosis; a way of knowing that comes out of the whole of you.

We find new answers and gain new wisdom as we open to expressing the truth of the pure essence of our soul. It is as if the light of our inner star begins to shine. Like the Star card in the Tarot: she is a symbol of personal truth, she is naked, real, grounded and cosmic at the same time as she waters the earth and is surrounded by stars.

Soul's glow has a magnetic quality and carries the power to attract. Like attracts like and its energy can draw others to you as you shine your light into the eyes of others and emanate energy waves of pure love. Love's energy can be contagious, so beware – you may infect others with feelings of happiness and joy that bubble up from within.

Courage is necessary if we are to claim our feminine power and it begins with being able to hold the creative possibility of miracles. We have taken the path into the darkness – facing fear and uncovering great riches of Hades/Pluto's realm.

Source is within you and resonates in your heart. Develop your own personal mythology and walk the mystical path. The prescription is to trust in your inner wisdom by valuing and loving the pure essence of who you are as a unique being; a small soul star with a glowing light that is waves of love twinkling brightly on our earth.

GIVE YOURSELF 8 CREATIVE GIFTS OF YOUR INNER CHILD

When you are real and true to yourself, you become free to live creatively as you reclaim the gifts of the inner child – gifts of openness, playfulness and joyful spontaneous wonder – as you experience each moment in time.

1. The gift of Presence to yourself as a physical being
2. The gift of Space to listen deeply to the voices of your soul
3. The gift of Time to be open to receive your soul's wisdom
4. The gift of Letting go and creating space for something new

5. The gift of Grounded connection to the world of nature and the Earth
6. The gift of Discovery, openness and willingness to be guided
7. The gift of Intuitive magic of thoughts from beyond your rational mind
8. The gift of Connection to the world of Cosmic Intelligence and Source

When clarity and self-confidence arrive, watch out world, here we come! We are no longer limited by our negative imaginations and the past choices we made. We now choose to become the Creatress of our unique soul story and our relationship to our soul has become the foundation for our happiness and fulfilment.

The secret to true happiness comes from living creatively and authentically in every moment, uncovering your gifts and sharing them in the world with kindness and grace.

Life becomes art as we learn to dance the sacred dance of soul, in tune with the core essence of our authentic self

A CREATRESS BLESSING

When you learn to tap into the mystery and magic of your feminine intelligence, you will find yourself empowered to make new choices and be guided to become the sacred dance and express the music of your soul. Colour the world with the beauty of your soul story.

On Angels wings

I breathe the Universe into me
I pause and hear the beat of my heart
And come to a place of stillness within
I breathe out with gentle flowing grace
Sending my love and caring into the world

I sit within my self and sense my soul
I am a star in the night sky
A bird that soars and lifts me high
My soul is both ancient and new
And I feel protected and loved

I embrace myself as a modern mystic

A Creatress Blessing

As I shape shift between two worlds
An angel wraps her wings around me
Wind caresses my wings and lets me fly
As if carried on Angels wings so high

I know that source is within me,
A peaceful place shows on my face
My heart is open and I glow with loving grace
My soul speaks my truth for others to feel
Let me walk the inner path so my soul may heal

Your soul knows how to lead you on what may seem to be a meandering pathway, so that you gather the experiences you need to create a foundation for you to create your unique soul story.

Steps down the Inner Path

Create space
And sit with silence
Step outside the familiar
Discover your inner truth
Use your imagination carefully
Seek hurt hidden beneath anger
Allow your creative inner child to play
The smallest step creates the greatest change
Uncover your gifts, they become your inner gold
Nurture yourself by hearing the calling of your soul
Heal your heart by healing your relationship to your self
As Creatress you manifest your life of abundance and joy

PART VIII

CREATRESS PRACTICES

Breathe is Life

There are many valuable ways we can train ourselves to strengthen our ability to live creatively and to reclaim the pure essence of the Feminine. Cosmic guidance comes through us in many subtle ways. Its truth awakens our heart and touches into our soul, opening us to guidance from the Creatrix and the intelligence of cosmic soul.

Creatress practices begin by supporting a deeper connection to our inner world and learning practical ways to expand our awareness of the subtle energies within that speak to us.

Taking time to breath into the moment and to allow space and time for something to grow out of the setting of a seed/an intention that may have come from an idea, an image, or a feeling

There are questions to be asked, lessons to be learned and a journey to be taken into the unknown realms of mystery; to retrieve the hidden parts of your inner self. When we take time out, to go within, to listen and learn to trust in soul messages as they reveal themselves to us. We develop the courage to believe in our inner wise self and learn to trust in the wisdom of our heart.

I have found these practices below helpful on my own soul journey, some of which are immense subjects in their own right. They are all ways of expanding consciousness to include the intelligence of the feminine perspective, awareness of subtle energies and consciousness of the invisible realms of soul:

Inner Work, Experiential Learning, Movement and Dance, Energy Healing, Meditation, Everyday Rituals, Art and Archetypes

Inner Work

Going on an inner Journey honours the whole energy system that is you. When we step outside of old patterning and focus within to create an honest relationship with ourselves, we find that this involves gaining new perspectives, changing values and learning new ways of listening as we tune into intuitive guidance that comes our way. To prepare to begin this inner journey we must first create an environment of trust and safety, so that we can become inner focused and breathe into our heart wisdom.

The attitude we bring to this inner work is also of importance. Setting clear intentions that resonate with your personal truth, showing kindness and grace towards yourself, and feeding yourself with loving respect, you value your inner world. This then allows you to become receptive to receiving wise guidance from your soul.

Trust: When we learn to trust in ourselves, we learn to trust the universe, so we are able to relax into becoming and able to extend kindness and grace to others.

Safety: Being grounded is to become fully present to ourselves as physical beings, so we can process our everyday experiences and feel supported by the earth beneath us. There are ways of becoming grounded that also bring us awareness of our whole energy body connection. They can be as simple as standing barefoot on the earth; or putting a thought form outside of our mind and onto paper; or expressing an emotion through a physical work of art. This not only makes it real by giving form to an experience, but also makes it possible for others to come into relationship with our experience.

Breath: Long, slow, deep, gentle breathing connects us to energy that is within us and all around us. It is a way of using the breath of life to focus energy and create a connection between the physical, the psychic and the cosmic dimensions of being.

Self-reflection: This involves questioning the overlay of accepted values that have been the norm for centuries, and have effectively devalued much that is feminine, including nature and the earth we live on. Self-reflection holds the power to lead us into awareness of our feminine intelligence, thereby gaining an expanded perspective on our lives.

Heart Wisdom: Feeling into heart wisdom brings emotions to

the surface to be recognised and acknowledged so that in time they can connect us to a sense of grace and healing.

Experiential Learning

It is too easy to become passive observers of life. To learn our soul lessons we need experiences that then create memories, which become stored in our bodies as a way of knowing in a felt sense that which is true for each of us. There are ways to honour your body wisdom that is vibrating with the energy of 'You' that heighten your sensitivity to energies and connect your physical body to your soul's presence.

The heart of this story as an inner quest for wholeness is to experientially explore the depths of yourself, learning to love the light and the darkness of your totality. Living as a Creatress requires us to reclaim spontaneous openness to psychic and intuitive knowing and trust in the playfulness innocence of our inner child.

Movement ~ Dance ~ the Rivers Flow

Our world is in constant movement as energy cycles continually unfold.

Mind and breath come together in the body with the movement of breath that connects us to the vibrations within us. As you move into each moment, notice the information you gain from that experience. You gain wisdom through your experiences of living ~ from thinking, to feeling, to doing, to being and becoming, and learning to dance to the music of your soul.

Movement ~Learning ballet. I began to learn ballet at the age of four and around the age of 15, I had a ballet master called Russell Kerr who would walk around with a stick he used to correct positions. I remember how he would hold my leg in arabesque, putting it into the position he wanted me to achieve so that my body could feel into this position and remember it. This created a body memory within me. It is through experiences of body memory that children learn to walk and talk. It is a whole body cellular way of learning that reverberates throughout our body and creates memories that resonate with our soul wisdom.

Movement is a way of re-membering the body's stored experiences of felt memory. Expression through movement can also become a way to ground a numinous experience so it is not lost and in time can blossom into an awakened insight that becomes new forms as expressed through ~ Journaling, Art, Music, and Dance. Expressions from our soul self include mind, emotions, and physical movement as a holistic expression of self.

Energy Healing

By shaping a new relationship to all that is the essence of the feminine, we develop energy awareness, from within and all around us that resonates with the beauty and truth that is the essence of our soul. Working with your energy body is a simple way to create a life of soul consciousness that is loving and wise, and uniquely your own.

Slow and listen and come into a relationship with your energy to gain consciousness of the energy of source by connecting with the intelligence of your emotions and your deep inner knowing.

As we learn to develop attunement to subtle energies by aligning the body to the rhythm of the soul, we honour natures power within us to balance and heal. Mind/Body practices help heal the Chironic split by grounding our experience in the physical and using vibrational healing to bring our knowing back into our bodies as a way of integrating our energy. Experiential mediums to work with our subtle energy body include image making, dream interpretation and dance.

These are some vibrational energy healing methods I have found useful: Reiki, Crystals, Essential Oils, Homeopathy and Flower Essences.

Reiki channels universal energy that enters the crown chakra moves down into the heart and sends healing energy out through the hands.

Crystals are tools that can increase your sensitivity to subtle energy vibrations by magnifying the energies within to awaken, balance and heal you.

Essential oils and Flower essences too attune to the energy vibrations of your essence and resonate with your soul. Essential oils can rapidly effect your emotional body and are thereby able to enhance your quality of life.

I use pure essential oils daily, knowing they utilise the vibrational powers of nature that can heal my psyche.

Homeopathy is where a minute substance is used, as like is used to treat like and thereby bring balance to the subtle body system.

Meditation

Meditation involves going beyond the restless, busy mind and entering into a deeper state – into the place of stillness and heightened consciousness. Some call this Mindfulness and yet to me meditation is the opposite of 'Mind Full' – it is the emptying of the mind, to be still and create a space and time to listen deeply, to become real and true to your inner self and open to the intelligence of Source.

Mindfulness practices as everyday rituals are exercises in presence. They still the mind and create a space to listen. There are some meditation practices include movement, such as yoga, Tai Chi and Qigong as ways of being present to our whole energy body. Through gentle movements we experience the flow of energy within and the ability to change our energy vibrations into a state of inner harmony by using these active forms of meditation

- Taichi
- Qigong
- Yoga
- Walking Meditation

I consider these practices a way of bringing me into a deeper awareness of the truth of myself as a dynamic energy body. This can also be achieved by becoming present in nature and grounded to the earth.

There are many Mindfulness practices being taught throughout the world and many programs, books and recorded meditations available.

I like to think of meditation as a doorway into finding ourselves and communing with our soul, more than as a passage of escape to lose ourselves to alluring dimensions of the beyond where we are no longer connected to the physical realm.

Here are a few of the meditation practices I have enjoyed: Buddhist meditations, Psycho-synthesis meditations and Joe Dispenza ~ *Breaking Habit of Being Yourself* meditations.

Everyday Rituals
~ Ways of Honouring the Sacredness of Life

Rituals can bridge the sacred space between the seen and the unseen worlds. They create a container for you to honour your experiences as a sacred act. This provides a connection to an expanded consciousness of your personal world and your place in it.

Let's not project our power outwards onto others but rather claim the wisdom and guidance that exists within us and find our way into a loving and creative life. Creatress Practices are any ritual that helps you go within and connect with your own inner wisdom, stored in your body as instincts, feelings, images, intuitive and psychic knowing. These practices can become everyday rituals and are a wonderful way of being able to ground our soul experiences.

Learning to live as a Creatress, your life becomes a soul practice. You become able to shift your attention easily between an inner and an outer focus. Trust in your feminine knowing creates a habit of showing yourself loving kindness and positive self-regard as an everyday way of living. Over time new habits become new rituals, as they become your new normal way of being as you honour the sacred in everyday life.

Group Rituals magnify the energy of the group to intensify each person's experience.

They have the power to reinforce experiential lessons so we are able to anchor the experience into our memory body in a way that honours the numinous quality of the original experience. Gathering together to raise the energy of the group lifts us into a heightened vibration that has the power to change our experience of ourselves to include the unseen mystery around us. Ancient Sharman used rituals to call up this sense of mystery and cosmic wisdom by joining together and singing, drumming, dancing, moving and awakening energy that resonates with our soul.

Retreats from our everyday life provide an opportunity to step outside of our lives and to visit somewhere new – mountains, forests, oceans, caves, walks in nature - to experience the unfamiliar and take the space and time just to be with ourselves. Any journey taken has the potential to open us to new ways of perceiving our lives. It is time spent invested in self-care that can restore harmony and balance to our soul. Good food, clean air, welcoming company and a container of safety creates an environment for us to explore our inner world and connect our body to our soul.

Yoga Retreat
Hot Spring Spas
Meditation Retreat
Experiential Workshops
Online Soul Gatherings

The Power of Art and Archetypes

Finding images that represent new energy coming into your life is a wonderful way to remind yourself so the memory of your experience is not lost; creating a treasure board as a way to capture inspiration by building up a collage of symbols that speak to your soul. Naming new archetypes empowers us and image making turns them into art.

Psycho-synthesis uses experiential sessions, where meaning is found through guided imagery journeying and then the experience is expressed by creating images.

Jungian psychotherapy uses dream work where meaning can be found by exploring symbols that arise from the dream world.

Dreams are the realm of imagination that speaks to us through images, words and emotions, often using symbols that resonate with our heart.

Sleep is a time when we commune with the unconscious realms and deep sleep is healing and empowering in the following ways:

- Integrating and healing by connecting the dots
- Expanding into other dimensions
- Letting go, being in the flow
- Restoring and healing the pain of hurt emotions
- Entering an invisible realm of mystery

- Connecting to wisdom – the intelligence of the cosmos.
- Awakening to knowing Cosmic Truth

> *To create a life of soul consciousness begins by showing kindness towards yourself and this leads to healing of your heart and your soul*

SOUL THERAPY FOR A CREATRESS

Your soul knows the truth of who you are and living a lie can make you unwell. It takes courage to become deeply honest with ourselves and to reach into the inner world where we hide our truth even from ourselves. By developing a greater awareness of the energy body of the self we open up to new choices and a rich quality of presence. This is where Soul Therapy involving Inner Work and Meditations can reveal your inner wisdom and bring you the healing experience of wholeness.

Becoming able to shift between inner focus and outer awareness is a skill that develops through practice, patience and loving kindness towards your self. This is part of becoming able to live a life guided by the wisdom of your soul.

This inner wisdom awakens us to the potential within each of us to create a new life story, one that is in alignment with the truth and beauty of our Soul.

To step into an empowered sense of self means to take on the mantle of a Creatress and own her power. Learn how to make every day sacred and to honour the mystery of life through Soul Therapy and giving herself Soul Health Days.

Simple Creatress Practices

- Breath is Life
- Waves on the Ocean
- Walking Meditation
- Soul Health Day

Breath is Life

Focusing on your breath is a powerful way to connect to the earth, the cosmos and to your sense of soul. In just a few moments of time you can slow down and connect within by choosing to breathe more deeply, slowly and more consciously. Breath is life and yet we so often take it for granted. When we become tense we find ourselves taking shallow breaths and then feel stressed and tired.

> Take time to be with yourself and begin to notice your breath. Start by breathing out as fully as you can and then pause before you take a deep slow breathe in. Take time to pause again before you let the next breath go. Before each new in breath it is important to pause, as this creates a space between the in and out breath.
> The out breath becomes the letting go of the old and then the pause becomes a preparation space before receiving the next new in-breath that is the breathing in the energy of that moment. By repeating this cycle of simple deep slow breathing three times you will find this brings you into deep relaxation, slowing and calming the brain as you enter into a relationship with your soul. When I simplify my life and take time to

breathe consciously, I create a sacred space to relax into and I open myself to guidance.

Meditation: Waves on the Ocean

When I meditate, I begin by noticing my breath and as I do I imagine it becoming waves of the ocean as I visualise the rise and fall of the tide washing over the sandy shore. As I observe my breath in this way it is as if I become one with the ocean of life.

Beginning by focusing on the out breath, I imagine letting go of the past. Freeing, releasing, lightening as I breathe out slowly. I pause in stillness and wait in this space until the next in breath presents itself. Taking a slow in breath, I imagine myself filling up with the energy of the moment and then I take time again to pause, waiting in stillness until the next out breath begins. I feel the graceful flow of water and as I continue this practice I feel the waves of the cosmos washing through me, cleansing, healing and releasing old energies to create space for the new to arise in me. I feel in harmony as I expand into becoming one with the ocean of life itself.

By using your breath to become more focused in this way, your life becomes an unfolding meditation as you creatively attune to the energies of each moment in time.

This brings you into your emotional body, allowing feelings to float up into your awareness. The trick is then to let them float away as you become the observer of your life rather than being enmeshed in it.

This letting go allows you to go deeper into your inner

depths to reveal more of the hidden depths beneath the surface of your everyday persona. You can use these practices at any time and for just a few minutes, when you need to breathe into a situation, to take a pause in your life and to see what unacknowledged truth is hidden within you.

I find both of these simple breath mediations are a way to be able to relax into yourself and to notice what is alive within you as information of your personal truth and a way into hearing inner messages.

Walking Meditation

I learned this active method of mediation many years ago at a Buddhist Meditation Retreat and it has stayed with me ever since. A walking meditation is one of the most powerful ways I know to bring me into a heightened awareness of my physical self. To take the time to be slow and to be inner and outer focused and to notice what arises from within as I take time to notice the hidden parts of myself.

> Begin by walking with bare feet and eyes in soft focus or closed depending on your situation. As you take a step, start to tune into yourself. Feel your breath as it enters and leaves your body and notice how deeply you allow your breath to reach into your body. Feel your feet as they meet with the ground and your weight, as it shifts from heel to toe. Feel the movements of all the bones and muscles and skin as they carry you through each step and your balance shifts as your foot meets with the earth beneath you. Take some time to be more conscious of each step by widening you focus to notice the movement in your legs, your hips and how you carry the weight of your body. This is a time for observing and being with yourself in the present moment. As you continue in your own rhythm of

walking, you will find yourself feeling into more and more of your physical presence and connecting to all that is the energy of you.

Time spent in meditation practice creates a field of energy that is receptive and connected with inner soul and outer cosmos. It is in this space, and the being in Kairos time that feeds our creative processes. Creating an emptiness, that is not empty, rather a space beyond conscious mind that is rich with potentiality and open to other dimensions that connect you to the intelligence of source.

Soul Health Day

A soul health day is a way to nurture and feed your soul on all levels of your being,
The best time to take a soul health day is at the time of the dark of the moon (when there is no moon visible in the sky) and you feel a natural desire to take time out from everyday life to retreat, to rest and to plant the seeds of new possibilities within the hidden mystery of your inner self. This dark of the moon is the perfect time for you to step out of your busy life. The aim is to spend time that is relaxed, open and receptive, a time to just be with yourself in what ever way that works for you. You can regard this as a time to be kind and loving to yourself and to invest in self-care, with good food, clean air and water and space and time just to be in relationship with yourself and the world around you. It may feel strange at first, especially if you hold the belief that your life is about caring for others and that the Me inside of you is not important enough to focus your attention on. Feelings of guilt may surface, and the fear of being alone can rise up to meet you as you take on this space within yourself.

The challenge is to develop positive self-regard. It starts with giving permission to your self to be still, quiet and receptive. This creates a space for you to be able to connect to your true essence, which is never lost. It is always there, waiting for you to hear its song calling you. By living in the moment, you give yourself time to commune with your soul which brings feelings that are peaceful, loving and joyful.

Listen to music, meditate, dance, paint a picture, write down any thoughts that inspire or inform you, or write a poem as words come to you.

Let your self express freely as you dance and sing and laugh and cry. Walk barefoot on the beach; watch the sun go down or the moonrise in the evening sky. Whenever I see the first crescent of the new moon in the sky I find myself taking a moment to make a wish; and I pause to breath deeply at the powerfully magnetic time when the full moon is present.

You may choose to relax around the house in your dressing gown if your everyday life requires you to wear formal clothes. Time spent with your hands in the earth, gardening or standing in a forest surrounded by tall tress can help to heal your feminine essence especially if you live in a crowded city. Or being beside a river watching the ever-moving force of the water's musical flow is nurturing if your life is usually controlled by rigid routines and expectations. This helps you to become in tune and own the rhythms of your energy. Time spent creating a garden is also time well spent in healing your feminine soul. This fosters a connection with nature and with the creative rebirth cycles of life itself.

> Prepare an altar with symbols to remind you of the
> sacredness of your everyday life resonating with
> the beauty of you truth.

Make your home into a sacred space.

Remember ~ How valuable is time spent in relationship to yourself, with an inner focus that connects you to the essential core of your soul. Your soul has gifts of truth and wisdom that can set you free to soar like a bird and return home again. Know that by valuing the diversity of our individuality in all its beauty and grace, we expand our experience of the depth and dimension of our own lives.

Honour the calling of your soul, as it resonates in your heart ~ Choose to become your authentic loving self

REMINISING'S

This book is the culmination of 70 years of 're-membering' myself, as an embodied soul on this earth in the dimensions of space and time. I write with words that come through me from the Creatrix and in my own words as I claim my voice. I find this gives new meaning to my life and I feel empowered to re-shape my world as an expression of my soul's truth.

I am now blessed with a quiet space and open-ended time to ponder and imagine as part of my creative process of writing. I have learned to not only ask clear questions but to be open to catching answers when they arrive, as they flash into consciousness, sometimes at inconvenient moments when I do not have pen and paper to hand. As the Creatrix speaks through me, I try to capture her essence in my poems with the words she has shared with me. Sometimes I lose all sense of time, as I become engrossed in the process of seeing the words unfold onto the page before me. I now live with her presence, as a quality of Being and I trust my inner wisdom as it guides me in each and every moment of my life.

I have learnt that it is the journey itself that becomes my life. So I now take time to enjoy the journey with all its twists and turns, its blocks and stagnant hollows and its ever flowing current that draws me along. I like to imagine life as a dance of ever changing energy, a constantly flowing river of forever unfolding movements.

There are times of deep sleep when I wake feeling heavy and deeply tired and I know I have been downloading information. Working on the psychic level can sometimes feel like one has run a long distance race and so I know that it is important to give myself time to relax and allow my physical energy body the time it needs to recuperate. Sleep to me is a valuable time for processing and restoring myself.

I notice that it was the smallest choices and steps taken that have had the greatest impact upon my life. Sometimes it was the briefest of meetings, a person who touched me on the level of my soul and then was gone, having left a memory in my heart forever. Some stories of brief moments in time:

Feeling the Breath of the Ocean ~ July 1989
    I have always loved the ocean, and especially when there are waves. This is a favourite place for me to meditate. Like the waves of the oceans, one night in France, the waves of the full moon's lunar energy washed through me, healing every cell of my body. I felt the waves of the cosmos as currents of love energy with the power to cleanse and heal me, changing me, awakening me to my passion for life itself. When we take

that passion and live creatively in each moment, the intelligence of the cosmos is always there to guide our way.

Meeting Emelie ~ May 1998

I remember sitting one evening on a balcony in Gothenburg, Sweden, looking at the full moon rising in the night sky and listening to the voices of people in the Italian restaurant below, and thinking to myself, "I had never dreamed of coming to Sweden, and yet here I am, sitting, knitting and waiting for my granddaughter to be born, a little flicka who was to be called Emelie. I was here waiting to meet a new soul with dark eyes and a knowing look, who would wind her self around my heart, reminding me of the sense of wonder and magic that comes with the creation of new life. Sometimes the dance of life takes us to places we never expected to be. We meet someone, experience something or learn something more fully by having had the experience. This has the power to change the shape of our lives forever.

A Dream and the symbol of a bird ~Feb 2019

I saw the most beautiful turquoise kingfisher sitting on the avocado tree, just outside my window. I had never seen one so large, or brilliantly coloured and sitting so close to me ever before in my life.

That night I dreamt that two large kingfishers flew into my house. They brushed against a glass window then they flew into other rooms before gracefully flying out the open door from which they had entered. I then remembered that earlier this night, two smaller birds had flown into my home. I am now unsure if I dreamed of the bird sitting on my avocado tree, as the lines between my dreaming and waking memories blur.

The kingfisher is my favourite bird. They like to live in the forest and to deep dive into rivers. Their colours are golden and turquoise blue and they are a symbol of good luck, abundance and joy for me.

I recall a visit long ago, to an island called Great Barrier, off the coast of New Zealand, which is isolated from much of the ways of our modern world. There are few cars on the island and visiting there can feel like stepping back in time. Everywhere I went I saw kingfishers dancing around in the air. I remember this as being a very special and magical place.

Quiet Night

I believe the Creatrix has been with me for a long time and her habit of speaking through me has taken over and directed my life for some time now. I have learned to trust in her voice, as her words come to me, for she has a soul story to tell. Often it is in the quiet stillness of the night that her words arrive flowing through my pen onto the paper that is always there in readiness on my bedside table. This night I heard these words -

> *"The inner voice of your soul will never*
> *ask of you to hurt another,*
> *For it is a loving voice that wants the very best*
> *for you and those around you.*
> *Your heart is the barometer of your soul's truth,*
> *Be still and listen, and feel into your open heart."*

Sacred Space

I have created a sacred space within my home to remind me of the sacredness within myself, choosing symbols that express my inner beauty and resonate with the beauty all around me. At times I add fresh flowers or an image from a tarot card or a colour I feel the need for at that time. But mostly in my sacred space there is a soft pink salt lamp, a feather the colour of a kingfisher, and an image of the Breakthrough Angel from the Angel Sanctuary in Alet les Bains, France; a crystal rock that holds a tea light candle; an image of a white flower bud, just opening with a sepia background and a diffuser for my essential oils and my most recent addition of a small blue glass bird, I call my bluebird of happiness, all set upon a white table. My chair is French style in old white with a velvet cover. The view outside my window is part of my sacred space also, with an avocado tree abundant with fruit, and the distant view of two extinct volcanoes, called Mount Victoria and Rangitoto Island. This space changes with the outer seasons reflecting changes within me.

The Magic of Dance

When my mother took me to my first ballet lesson. From the very first moment I knew that I had found something that I loved to do. From that time onwards, something inside of me had changed. I danced on the beach every summer and I danced in my mind before I went to sleep every night. Whenever I danced I felt my movements were graceful and free, filling me with feelings of happiness. My heart would sing and I felt like a bird soaring high. It was through this experience of dancing, I found a joy that has never left me. My happy place as a child was whenever I was dancing. I still remember the

French words for the ballet steps and I keep fond memories of my dancing alive.

When you find your happy place, go there often. Speak kindly and lovingly to yourself and trust in the wisdom of your soul. Feed your relationship to your inner self and it will reward you with a world that reflects this confident, loving self, back to you.

My whole life has become a dance and I look for the poetry in everything as witness to the beauty and grace with which life unfolds before me. That, to me, is what living as a Creatress is about, living in the moment, connected to my inner wisdom. Looking back over those years of questing for insight, inspiration and inner wisdom. I realise the answer was there all the time; I only needed to hear the voices of my soul speaking its wisdom to me, to learn to trust in her guidance and to be willing to courageously walk my own path as it revealed itself before me and to be able to find the gift of freedom to be authentically me.

When you deeply love yourself
You find yourself in love with life
Then you will see love everywhere
Love is the energy that connects us all
It is the source energy of the boundless universe

Our Soul's story needs to be experienced by delving into the darkness of the realms of mystery within us and by facing our fears and moving through them into a heart space that is graceful and loving. For me this has meant owning the Persephone woman within me and living my life as a modern mystic.

Feel the freedom of being in love with life and creatively living in the flow. Express your gifts and feel the joy that follows, as you become a glowing soul connected to the beauty and truth that is **y**our unique and authentic soul self.

*"True knowing comes from the world of cosmic intelligence,
And our soul's truth that is uniquely ours to own."*

My hope is that my story will inspire you to awaken the unique sparkle of your truth, to hear the voices of your Soul, to follow your heart and to Love the truth and beauty of yourself as a Modern Mystic and a Soulful Creatress.

And then you can say -

*"I'm feeling immense joy and happiness in my life,
And I believe in magical moments"*

ACKNOWLEDGMENTS

Thanks to the writers whose work inspired me and encouraged me to believe in my feminine self.
Marion Woodman for her illuminating books on feminine consciousness ~ Including *The Pregnant Virgin*.
Other Jungian writers who took Jung's psychology to another level by including the feminine perspective; Jean Shinoda Bolen, Linda Schierse Leonard and many more.

A special thank you to Lynda for her support in this project and Marnie for being there, for keeping me tech savvy and assisting me in a myriad of ways; and Franchelle for her encouragement and feedback on my first draft.

My appreciation goes to Penelope Carroll for her insightful contribution as editor.

And finally my gratitude goes to the Creatrix for gifting me to become a channel for her soul messages.

SOURCES AND OTHER READING

Bolen, Jean Shinoda
Goddesses in Everywoman,
A New Psychology of Women.
Harper & Row Publishers, Inc. 1985

Cameron, Julia
The Vein of Gold,
A Journey to Your Creative Heart
Pan Books, 1997

Dispenza, Joe
Breaking the Habit of Being Yourself
Hay House, Inc. 2012

Downing, Christine (Edited by)
Mirrors of the Self
Archetypal images that shape your life
St Martin's Press. 1991

Ferrucci, Piero

What We May Be: Techniques for Psychological and Spiritual Growth Through Psycho-synthesis.
Jeremy P. Tarcher, Inc. 1982

Leonard, Linda Schierse
The Wounded Woman
Healing the Father-Daughter Relationship
Shambhala Publications, Inc. 1982

Luke, Helen M.
The Way of Woman
Awakening the Perennial Feminine
Doubleday, 1995

Luke, Helen M.
Women: Earth and Spirit,
The Feminine in Symbol and Myth
Crossroad Publishing Co, New York. 1981

Myss, Caroline
Sacred Contracts,
Awakening Your Divine Potential
Bantum Books, 2001

Pearson, Carol S.
Persephone RISING
Awakening the Heroine Within
Harper Elixir 2015

Tolle, Eckhart
Practicing The Power of Now,
A Guide to Spiritual Enlightenment
New World Library 2001

Woodman, Marion

The Pregnant Virgin,
A Process of Psychological Transformation.
Inner City Books, 1985

Woodman, Marion & others
Leaving My Father's House
A Journey to Conscious Femininity
Shambhala Publications. 1992

ALSO BY MADELINE K. ADAMS

Odyssey of a Creatress
~ A Heroine's Journey to Uncover
The Essence of Her Feminine Soul

Soul Star ~ Child of the Universe
~ Soul Poems and Heart Wisdom

Below is the link to Madeline's Amazon Author page
www.amazon.com/author/madelinekadams

Visit her Soul Community
www.sourceandsoul.com

Visit Madeline's website ~ for Soul Star magic
www.madelinea.com

POSTSCRIPT

Many of us have been hiding, not speaking, living in the shadows of others, holding fears connected to ancient unforgotten and disempowering memories, and past traumas: from the devaluing of Mary Magdalene to the witch-hunts of old, there is much to be questioned and much to be redefined.

Now is the time for new empowering feminine archetypes to become visible in this Aquarian era. I will explore more of these in my next book in the Source and Soul Series.

ONE LAST THING.....

If you enjoyed this book or found it useful, I'd be very grateful if you'd post a short review at your preferred retailer. Your support really does make a difference and I read all the reviews personally.

Thanks for your support!

ABOUT THE AUTHOR

Madeline K Adams is an intuitive, a dancer and seeker of soul. She has a B. Com. degree with postgraduate studies in psychology and thirty years experience in astrology.

She writes from her unique perspective capturing simple truths and cosmic wisdom in words that she hopes will resonate with your heart. She re-defines feminine archetypes as a Creatress, Persephone woman and Modern Mystic.

Madeline's vision is to inspire others to walk the inner path, a journey deep within to become a seeker of soul. She believes it is our feminine intelligence that holds the key to bring healing and balance to our selves, others, and our world.

This her second book *The Sacred Dance of Soul* is about feminine empowerment; to know the inner power of our soul that resides within us all. Life becomes Art as we learn to dance in tune with the pure creative essence of our soul.

Madeline resides in Auckland, New Zealand. She lives as a Creatress in her own unique Aquarian way, guided by the creative intelligence of her soul.

Connect to her Community ~ For Inspiration and updates on her upcoming books ~ Visit her websites
www.madelinea.com
www.sourceandsoul.com

 facebook.com/soulstarmagic

www.ingramcontent.com/pod-product-compliance
Lightning Source LLC
Chambersburg PA
CBHW021951290426
44108CB00012B/1024